D0848013

COURTESY

PETER CANINE

PER

CHUCK DAY
3/9/22

I SAW LEN PLAY
MANY TIMES -
GREAT GUY &
PLAYER
TRAGIC ENDING

LESSONS FROM LENNY

THE JOURNEY BEYOND A SHOOTING STAR

Tony Massenburg & Walt Williams

Library of Congress Control Number: 2018905679
ISBN: 978-0-9995320-0-3

Published in the United States of America by
Whyde Range Productions, LLC
12598 Ridgely Road, Suite 4
Greensboro, MD 21639
www.WhydeRangeProductions.com

PHOTO CREDITS
Courtesy of University Archives,
University of Maryland Libraries

Book design by Adam Robinson and Spencer Thompson
for Good Book Developers

Printed in the United States of America

CONTENTS

To the family of Len Bias, our loved ones,
and the survivors.

—Tony Massenburg and Walt Williams

Foreword

GARY **WILLIAMS**

Naismith Memorial Basketball Hall of Fame Coach

I only wish I could have coached Tony Massenburg for more than just one year. Tony performed as well as any player in the ACC my first year at Maryland. He did everything we needed on the court and in the locker room as a senior captain because he would not give in or give up. I cannot think of anyone who went through more than Tony did in a college career. He played for "Lefty" Driesell, Bob Wade, and me. Having just one coaching change is difficult in itself but to have three different college coaches and still make the necessary adjustments to succeed within each program is a testament to his character. To get where he did as a basketball player during that time, then having a long career in the NBA and winning a World Championship, I think Tony is a great role model for young players. He's living proof that if you are willing to work hard, you can make really great things happen.

Walt Williams was very influential in my ability to stay at Maryland for twenty-two years, and he deserves to be credited for providing a bridge and a foundation for us to build a championship program. Once the sanctions hit us in 1990, Walt could have left the school and played for any team of his choice; he chose to stay, which I will always respect, and his decision made us at least competitive and resulted in two great recruiting classes that helped us turn the program around. After Walt's last game, I told him what Maryland Basketball becomes will be a direct result of his dedication to the University. He gave us the stage to reach the top. Walt had a tremendous career at Maryland and was a lottery pick when he finished. He also established a scholarship in honor of his father not long after being drafted, which I think says a lot about who he is, and went on to enjoy a lengthy NBA career as "The Wizard."

Tony and Walt graduated from Maryland but they never left the program. Their presence on campus and in the community remains such a positive force. They were leaders on my first team at Maryland and no team of mine fought harder. Things weren't so good for us in 1989 when we came together. There were no rivals, but nobody played with more purpose than we did. That determination sets a tone, and the resolve it takes to win against the odds is something I referenced to each of my teams as we worked our way into a championship program. It all started with that first team, led by Tony and Walt. The special thing is they carried it beyond winning basketball games. The loyalty and commitment they demonstrate to the University of Maryland and the Maryland basketball program is invaluable. As coaches, we want our players to excel as student-athletes and grow into successful citizens. Tony and Walt refused to allow hardship and loss to hold us or them back. Maryland needed student-athletes like Tony and Walt to survive devastating circumstances and the University continues to benefit from their example. It's just great to see them doing so well in their lives. They make great messengers of the lessons going forward.

LESSONS FROM LENNY

THE JOURNEY BEYOND A SHOOTING STAR

Spring, 1986

Leonard "Len" Bias, from Landover, Maryland, a two-time Atlantic Coast Conference (ACC) Player of the Year and All-American basketball star at the University of Maryland, is the number two overall pick in the National Basketball Association (NBA) draft.

Tony Massenburg, from Sussex County, Virginia, is an eighteen-year-old scholarship player on the University of Maryland basketball team.

Walt Williams, from Prince George's County, Maryland, is a sixteen-year-old sophomore on the Crossland High School varsity basketball team, 13 miles from the University of Maryland.

Chapter 1

THE **DREAM**

"The Boston Celtics select Len Bias of the University of Maryland."

—David Stern, Commissioner, National Basketball Association, June 17, 1986

TONY MASSENBURG

Lenny dreamed of being drafted by Boston. We talked about the three-year courtship and the Celtics trading with the Seattle Supersonics in 1984 to acquire a future first-round pick. We all knew Lenny had a great time at a camp for kids in New England with Arnold "Red" Auerbach, the Celtics' President, how they admired each other, and how much he enjoyed the championship environment and being around the Celtics.

Three weeks before the draft, Lenny told us to look for him in the Boston Garden during the 1986 NBA Finals and there he was on TV, sitting courtside, tuned-in to the Celtics bench, reading the players and coaches. He looked ready to check in for someone at the next whistle.

In our final pickup game before he left for the draft ceremonies in New York, Lenny made the first shot and as the ball snapped the nets he yelled, "Bird for three," giving a shout out to Celtic Hall of Famer Larry Bird, just one of the legends he wanted to join. Throughout our year together, Lenny was more

and more certain that Boston was the perfect fit and the rest of the team agreed. Everyone thought the Bias-to-Boston deal was a lock so most of our pre-draft chatter centered on the type of suit he would wear when he stepped on stage to greet the NBA Commissioner and sparkle in the bright lights where he clearly belonged.

Pickup basketball was such an enormous part of playing at Maryland and, in those last games, Lenny glided up and down the court like an Olympic speed skater, effortless, majestic, and dominant. Each one of us picked up on his spirit and tried to play the same way: smooth, sharp, and perfect.

At the end of the day's final game, I crashed the boards to grab a rebound and jumped into an off-balance, left-handed, put-back dunk for the win. The big throwdown set off a round of emphatic "oohs" and "awws" from the team with Lenny screaming, "Yea, Big Young'un," his nickname for me. He hustled to pick the ball up, palmed it with his left hand, made a comical face imitating my in-flight grimace, leaned into the group like he was dunking on us, and let out a monster growl before cracking up laughing. Everyone joined in the laughter and I was as happy as anyone because it was funny, because Lenny was funny. But it was so much more because we knew what Lenny was saying with his gentle mockery: "All right, little brother, I see you climbing. I see you in the weight room. I see all the work you're putting in, and big brother approves."

The pats on the back and the "you should have seen your face" needles in my side kept us shoulder-bumping all the way to the locker room, glad to be brothers, teammates one last time. If anyone had been there to see, we must have looked like kids heading into school from recess going over the highlights of another great day on the playground, happy to relive the last game and looking forward to the next in the sort of everlasting summer of basketball and friends that we loved when we were kids.

This is why I wanted to go to the University of Maryland, to spend my freshman year in the Len Bias family and rejoice across the court the way I'd watched the 1984 ACC champion Terps

celebrate, to learn what it takes to be "The Man," and follow him into the NBA. I fell asleep the night before the '86 NBA draft thinking of all that joy, of being on my way, of being just like Lenny.

WALT WILLIAMS

At sixteen, life seems sweet. I was a sophomore on the Crossland High School basketball team, and we'd just won the 1986 Maryland State Championship title—a game played on the famed Cole Field House floor. It's still clear and fresh in my mind, dancing from one end of the court to the other, a state champion in the tenth grade, and what made it most precious was the thought of being on the sacred hardwood where Len Bias, "The Man," had dominated opponents and brought the fans to their feet for four years.

Sixteen is a highly impressionable age, and, for a sixteen-year-old in the "DMV," as every local basketball player called the District of Columbia, Maryland, and Virginia region, basketball was what we lived, basketball stars were who we admired, and college basketball the world we dreamed of joining.

What a star-studded world it was back then.

The Georgetown Hoyas were among the nation's best teams by the mid-80s and the Maryland Terrapins had the best player in the country. In those years, when my time was spent either practicing or playing pickup and my mind was consumed with basketball, Len Bias exploded on the scene as the most impressive, dominating player in college hoops. I had a local sports hero to emulate, an idol from the same streets I played on, and it focused my attention, ignited my passion, and hardened my determination to play my best every day, every game. Superstars and nationwide favorites Julius "Dr. J" Erving and Kareem Abdul-Jabbar seemed to exist in some unattainable basketball Mount Olympus, but I knew that "The Man," Len Bias, was a homeboy from Prince George's County, Maryland, just like me, and now he was the greatest player in the country.

I still remember the first time I saw him play. It was a snowy night in 1983 and the awesome Adrian Branch dominated the action. Toward the end of the game, Branch passes to a player cutting baseline wearing a number thirty-four jersey. With his back to the basket, number thirty-four gathers the assist and simultaneously spins into the prettiest turn-around jumper imaginable. That picture-perfect number thirty-four jersey levitates a full body length higher than the defender, the ball travels an exact arc through the absolute center of the hoop, and down to the floor without even brushing the net.

My father and I looked at each other, wide-eyed and amazed with our jaws dropping. We talked Terps all the way home and then watched the local news programs to catch the latest about the Hoyas, and to see if the highlight segment on the Terrapins captures us among the Cole Field House crowd. The Hoya report focuses on Patrick Ewing and Georgetown's drive for a national championship. Adrian Branch from renowned DeMatha Catholic High School headlines the Maryland video package. The last piece of footage from Cole Field House spotlights number thirty-four running down the court after making a basket, with the name Len Bias and Northwestern High School spelled out underneath.

At that moment, Len Bias snags the spot in my heart that every true fan has reserved for a favorite player. I liked the name Bias, that jump shot deserved a patent, and the Northwestern High School reference introduced an exciting concept. The Crossland High School Cavaliers played the Northwestern Wildcats regularly during the season and we'd teamed up with and against one another on the same playgrounds and in the same recreation centers since we first managed to get a ball up to the basket.

Learning the number thirty-four Terrapin with the sweet jump shot, Len Bias, emerged from a Prince George's County public high school was like discovering a long-lost member of the family, a big brother. DeMatha High School, also a Prince George's County institution, is still the best of the private schools and a national power, and for the select few. Witnessing a Prince George's County public school kid on television playing for the home team gave me a powerful sense of pride and marked the onset of my recruitment to College Park.

Growing up a Washington Bullets fan and cheering for Georgetown was just the way it was in P.G. County, and the fact that each team had rosters packed with future stars curbed the impulse to identify with one player. But, now it was different.

If Len Bias could make it from Northwestern, I knew a kid from Crossland could make it too. Out of the blue, Len Bias rose in the public imagination the same way he rose over his opponent and shot that jumper and he became the inspiration and idol of a generation of public school players. Sure, I kept tabs on Georgetown, but more and more I watched the sports highlights to see number thirty-four and the Terps. I fell deeper in love with the game, his game.

I developed a bias.

So, I set out to be like Len. I wanted to be as good, as tight, and as smooth as Len Bias. Following his example on the court became my sole focus. In the parks, on the blacktop, I tried to play like Len Bias. As Len ascended toward a place on the Mount Rushmore of Maryland Basketball, the ladder extended down to my reaching hands. I knew I could grab that first rung and climb if I kept working to win every challenge every day.

In 1984, Georgetown took "March Madness" by storm and walked off with the National Championship. Everyone in the "DMV" had champions to cheer for: local, national, and Olympic. Basketball was the king of our sporting lives, competition and trash-talking on our streets and playgrounds grew fierce, and bragging rights ranked supreme. All my friends wore Georgetown shirts and jackets and plastered their walls with clippings of legendary Hoyas like David Wingate and Reggie Williams.

Although Wingate and Williams have Maryland roots, the player winning over my heart grew up only a few miles from me, and "The Man from Landover" delivered a Most Valuable Player performance to win the ACC championship, which felt like a national title, giving me reason to believe I can make it from the humble P.G. County hardwoods. To make up for lost time, I played basketball on every court I could get to, following the momentous popularity of Len Bias and the sport of choice in the "DMV." My plan was to master the fundamentals as a freshman and splash down at Crossland High School as a member of the varsity in my sophomore season. I had a plan, I had a goal, and a teenager with those things can do almost anything.

Len Bias bridged a divide between two worlds. Most kids in and around my community rooted for Georgetown. The Maryland Terrapins appealed more to our neighbors to the north. Rarely did I see someone on the playground wearing Terrapin gear until Len Bias changed everything.

Everyone in the "Free State" cheered for "The Man from Landover." We united aboard the Maryland flagship to marvel at a shooting star going supernova. Len Bias raised "DMV" fan appreciation for Maryland Terrapins basketball to equal the national powerhouse Georgetown Hoyas. Len shines and connects Terp fans who cheered for the great Tom McMillen with a basketball-crazed region of urban youth, freeing us to walk tall in our Maryland gear right down the streets of Georgetown—smooth and easy. Len Bias moved Marylanders to celebrate the Terrapin that lived inside them. Because of "The Man," I realized I was a Terp.

Len's national "coming-out party" was the 1984 Atlantic Coast Conference Tournament. He exploded: scoring, rebounding, running the court, and dominating so completely that, after Maryland beat Duke University in the final, there was no way he wasn't going to be named Tournament MVP. That game was big time on the playgrounds of the "DMV." We had a champion, and I was sure anyone who paid attention to college basketball had to be a Len Bias fan by the end of the tournament. The upset of Georgetown by the Villanova Wildcats in the 1985 NCAA Championship, and the crowning of Len Bias as the ACC Player of the Year, spurred more and more rangy, high-leaping kids out to the playgrounds to mimic "The Man." Len was always there, an inspiration in the heart, like when a ball swishes through the net after a high-arching jump shot and the shooter calls out "Bias!" as he back-pedals down court. It was a testimony, a pledge that the boy is trying to be like "The Man."

In February of 1986, the memorable clash between the Terps and the Tar Heels of North Carolina showcased an all-time great Len Bias performance, perhaps the best of his career, an instant classic, a game that continues to resonate across the basketball world. To a young number one fan of "The Man," Bias giving the new Dean E. Smith Center its first defeat carried special significance.

I'm in North Carolina on the floor of my aunt's bedroom watching the second half of that unforgettable contest alone to escape the chatter and howls of a house filled with Tar Heel followers. When the game ended, my cackling cousins were quiet. Bias silenced them. Out of respect, I kept my cool but I wanted to scream, "Len Bias! Maryland! What?"

Bias lifted me and Maryland so high I could only see one way: Be Like Len. The overtime win over number one North Carolina elevated Len Bias beyond ACC Player of the Year to near "Dr. J" status but I saw "The Man," a lanky kid from P.G. County, mesmerizing the nation, sending tremors through the "Dean Dome" and rocking Tobacco Road. I remembered some of the older guys at the park calling me "lanky" and I thought, "I *can* be like Bias."

Suddenly there was talk of a P.G. County public school student-athlete playing in the NBA and some of the sportswriters saying he might be the best player ever. It almost sounded like the stories kids make up to prop up their city, their cousin, or the star player on their high school team. The golden doors of "The League" opened only for a select few and, usually, the sort of supermen who were known by a single name like "Bird," "Kareem," and "Magic." Those guys were born and raised in a different world and destined to play at a higher level and surely a higher altitude than mere mortals.

Len gave precious hope to youngsters in every corner of the Washington, DC region, living proof that a kid from our streets could be the best, all the way to the NBA. "The Man" opened a door to opportunity where previously there was only a stone wall. Because of Len Bias, I grew optimistic and determined. I believed, without a doubt, if he could, I could as well.

It's the 1986 Maryland High School State Championship and I'm in the lay-up line inside Cole Field House, in awe, heart racing, set to wind up my sophomore season as a champion. Being there to play, like a Terrapin, with a game tape of Maryland Basketball streaming through my head and "The Man" in the building to watch, feels as if a genie had granted my one wish. The Crossland High veterans—Mike White, Keith Williams, Mike Sumner, Aaron Martin, and Clarence Alford—carried us to victory. As we bounced around the court in the postgame dance of triumph and joy, I imagined it was almost like Len's outstanding second season at Maryland, the year he blossomed from a skinny sophomore to a national icon. In that magical madness, how could I not think that I could do it too? The flash of the championship team photograph gave me an afterimage of a future picture, one where I'm in Cole Field House as a Terp, surrounded by my Maryland teammates.

Standing inside Cole and looking around, I felt like the present happened a long time ago. It was the strangest feeling. The photographer barked at us to straighten up, the mental picture faded, and I snapped back to being a sophomore champion, one of the kings of P.G. County.

Like Len.

My high school teammates depended on me to grow into a key performer as we fought to defend our state title in my junior season. I placed the championship trophy on the shelf in April of 1986 and fought my limitations as much as any opponent. I vowed to upgrade an aspect of my game each and every day. At night, I studied and watched the evening and late-night sports shows for talk about Len and the NBA, crafting a boy's dream into a man's ambition. During storm-interrupted afternoons, I practiced shooting by lying on my bedroom floor and aiming at a barely visible spot on the ceiling.

Two months later, I'm on the floor looking up but the dot has faded under a pool of tears as Len's death at twenty-two broke my heart.

Len Bias pulled me forward. Every accolade he received was one I could aim for. He heightened my imagination and strengthened my expectations of achievement. He'd been the ultimate P.G. County champion, the best player Maryland has ever seen, and as the different images of Bias in action slide across my mind's eye, I hear my voice saying, "I'm going to be like him." The pain was almost purifying as I fell asleep alternately crying and swearing to make it to Maryland, because he lived.

Because he died.

We heard through the grapevine early on Lenny's draft day that the Celtics chose him with the second pick. We hugged and high-fived and couldn't wait until the evening to see Lenny step into "The League" on cable TV. Then we did what all Terps did: we went to the courtyard to put up jump shots, have a dunkfest, and

in our way, celebrate our guy making the dream come true, not just his dream but all our dreams.

We made it! We were in "The League."

Around seven o'clock on draft night, we gathered at the home of Dervey Lomax, the former Mayor of College Park, to watch TBS show Lenny crossing over from college star to NBA celebrity. There he was, on the biggest stage of his life, of any of our lives, looking silky in an off-white suit, sharp and relaxed, with the green Celtics cap matching his outfit like a fashion model. We cheered just like the fans that filled Cole Field House for every game.

He made it.

We made it.

Star point guard Keith Gatlin drove us back to campus and we speed-walked to the suite he shared with Lenny in Washington Hall, knowing it wasn't likely but still hoping "The Man" would decide to spend his first night in "The League" at home. The suite was empty, so we figured he was with his family, and I skipped to my dormitory. I was sure he'd be back after breakfast, strolling into Cole Field House, arms filled with Reeboks for everyone, and ready for the afternoon pickup games with his boys.

This wouldn't be the normal bumping and grinding with Lenny the two-time Player of the Year anymore; it would be my first time defending "The Man" who'd made it to "The League." Just the anticipation of competing with a Boston Celtic made me a better player. The tune whistling through my head was, "I play with Lenny Bias which means I can play and I'm going to play with Lenny all summer, every summer, and everywhere he works out, maybe with his Boston teammates, maybe at the All-Star game."

Lenny lived the dream but it was my dream as well. I lived in College Park, Maryland, home of the brightest star in college basketball, the greatest place on earth.

Pickup games started early on the day after the Celtics selected "The Man," but we were looking at the clock more than we were keeping score. Before each game, guys taking warm-up shots trotted around the court with an eye on the back doors of

Cole Field House, hoping that at any moment those doors would slam back and Lenny would walk in, in Celtic Green, ready to play and give us the scoop on Boston and the Big Apple.

It was not to be.

The sun set on Wednesday, June 18 and Lenny still hadn't appeared. We agreed he was somewhere in the big time: hanging with Bill Russell or touring Boston's streets with K.C. Jones. Perhaps he'd been called to a photo shoot with Earvin "Magic" Johnson and Michael Jordan or hopped on a private jet to film a music video with Janet Jackson in Beverly Hills.

We joked about him becoming so popular, we'd never see him again. As it turned out, I never did.

Chapter 2

THE **NIGHTMARE**

"He's gone."

—Mrs. Lonise Bias, June 19, 1986

TONY

I felt scared in the final moments of sleep on the morning of June 19, 1986. The sound of my teammate, David Gregg, beating on my door echoes into the end of an icy-cold dream I can never quite remember. A stream of light shooting through the gap under the door flickers with the shadow of David's movements. He's sliding from side to side.

The banging turns desperate and I'm at the door in a blink. This isn't just David fooling around. I focus, turn, and yank the door knob. As I pull it, David falls forward into my room, grabs my arm, and tries to tell me something. He's so frantic and I'm so woozy from my strange dream that his words run together like an auctioneer in a horror movie. He darts back and forth still talking at top speed, and through a groggy, semiconscious fog, I hear "Lenny," "seizure," and "Leland Hospital."

None of his words sink in but a trembling, incoherent David bouncing off the walls at the break of dawn does. Something is wrong, terribly wrong. David dashes out of my room in Allegany Hall as I try to piece together the situation while I rush to throw

on some clothes. The sound of fists hammering on other doors turns the suite into a madhouse.

"A seizure?" All I could think of was uncontrollable shaking and eyes rolling backwards.

"Epilepsy?" No, that couldn't be Lenny.

What the hell was really going on?

In the hall, fellow freshman Dave Dickerson and I shouted questions to each other.

"What did David say?"

"Could Lenny have had a seizure?"

"When did Lenny come home?"

"Did you see him?"

There were many questions and no answers. Leland Memorial Hospital was about the only fact either of us knew for sure so we sprinted to my two-seater and, with Dickerson navigating and me cutting corners and slamming through the gears, we made the eight-minute journey to the hospital in five. All the way, we were still spinning possibilities without facts. Nothing made any sense. Lenny's body was a precision machine.

A seizure?

Maybe he was allergic to something. Sure! They probably served crabs and seafood up at the ceremony. The doctors will prescribe medicine to control the symptoms and everything will be fine.

Food poisoning?

Sure! A bad tray of appetizers slipped in while Lenny was sampling the high life after the NBA draft festivities. That explains why we didn't see him on Wednesday and why we didn't get the dish on Larry Bird and all the other legends in the Celtics' Hall of Fame.

He got sick on the airplane flying back to Maryland!

That's why we didn't see him. He must have been sick, and tired, and his body just rejected a raw fish or a rare steak.

It's a seizure. Kids have seizures.

It's epilepsy. He just needs the right medicine.

The five minutes of high-speed best-case speculation keeps us from going crazy but I can't forget the horrified look on David Gregg's face. He looked like a ghost.

We arrive at the hospital and the guessing game, the anxious grasping for hope is over.

Dickerson is out of his seat before my car even stops rolling, fast-walking to the front doors.

I can't move. I've got the steering wheel gripped so hard my fingers feel stuck. I'm afraid to let go, afraid to get out of the car and into a world of harsh truth. In my head, I see Lenny smiling so big in his new Celtics cap. I can hear his booming voice joking and laughing in the locker room. I remember leaping from the bench as he dunked backwards to seal the big win against North Carolina. I've heard people say life can flash before your eyes during a crisis. I was in a trance with spinning images of Lenny Bias in the seconds I sat frozen in my car.

I'm shaking but I finally get out. Leland looks like a clinic, not a hospital. This wouldn't be where they'd take Lenny if he needed emergency care. My aching mind tries to tell me he must be okay or we'd be going to a "real" hospital downtown in DC.

It's quiet. I spot an unmarked police car parked near the entrance.

There's movement behind the glass doors and teammates Jeff Baxter and Keith Gatlin walk out, talking intensely. Keith has his hands on top of his head, and Jeff is pinching his brow. They see us coming and a single glance at their agonized faces tells me whatever is happening is not good.

This seizure thing must be severe.

We hustle through the entryway into a waiting area and find our teammates scattered around the room, faces filled with fear and worry. Still without facts, the "What happened?" conversation goes around and around the group mixing with gasps and sighs of frustration and pain. I try to stop and talk to everyone, trying to give a little comfort, trying to find all the comfort I can get, trying to squeeze my fears into hope.

For what seems like forever, there are no facts, just endless speculation. Nothing makes any sense. We're caught in the trap of "no news is good news" and a forced optimism evolves into confidence. Whatever ails Lenny will be temporary and insignificant. It just has to be.

No seizure is going to prevent Lenny from walking out with us. After all, he's "The Man." Everything he's ever done has made him bigger, better, stronger, and more miraculous than anyone else. How could a seizure, mysterious and fearsome as it might be, bring him down?

The possibility that Lenny might die never enters my mind. First off, young men like us are immortal and second, I've idolized Lenny for three years and after twelve months in the gym running and lifting with the best athlete in college basketball, I knew Lenny Bias was invincible.

A seizure is scary but certainly survivable.

Mrs. Bias hurries into the hospital and down the hallway with the doctors to see about her son. Every minute until she returns feels like an hour. Without warning, the doors swing open and pushes a breeze across my face I can still feel today. As Mrs. Bias walks toward us, anticipation drains the last drop of the adrenaline that's responsible for keeping me from breaking down. Frozen for three anxious seconds as I read her body language, I see the mother of my friend, composed, and prepared to alleviate the rampant fear petrifying the waiting area.

Standing to hear Mrs. Bias speak, I whispered a simple prayer: "Please let Lenny be okay."

Mrs. Bias opens her arms and clearly says, "He's gone."

She speaks with a calm demeanor and a peaceful presentation that gave me a moment of relief. I misinterpreted her deliverance. I thought "gone" meant transferred to another hospital or "gone" to sleep because of the medication. One second passes while the doubt and confusion about what she has just said stirs within me. The next second stopped time. "Lenny is GONE" hits and temporarily shuts down all five senses. Shock scrambles my mind and body and I can't breathe. Nothing moves. My friend cannot die.

I'm only eighteen.

I dropped into a chair as the walls collapsed around us. The pain pierced the nerves in my chest, I buried my head in my hands, and a tone rang in my ears like the steady sound of a heart monitor when life ends. Nothing else said in the waiting area sticks, only the two words from Mrs. Bias mixing with the metaphoric tone.

News of Lenny being rushed to the hospital went viral without the Internet or Twitter, and the media lining up near the entrance prevented Dickerson and me from running out to find air. Dave put his arm around me as we turned to re-enter the lobby and his heart pounding on my shoulder proved the nightmare was real. Lenny Bias is gone forever, along with the life we enjoyed and expected.

I looked back at the waiting area through tear-soaked palms and a chaotic scene of teammates in misery burns into the core of my memory, a horrendous contradiction of our year together. This cannot happen.

The final words were said. The Bias family left to share their pain in private and those of us stuck in Leland Memorial were left numb, knowing the nightmare will last forever.

Lenny Bias was dead.

Gone.

It was hard to breathe the day Lenny died, as it has been at some point of every day for more than thirty years as I face the melancholy reminders that are a permanent byproduct of losing a brother far too soon. The weight of reality closed my eyes and took me back to a better place and time, to the back seat of our family car, traveling down Interstate 95 after visiting College Park and a younger self explaining to my parents why visiting any other school was just a waste of time. My mind was made up.

I wanted to play at the University of Maryland with the great Lenny Bias.

WALT

The Bias family and the Terrapin players waiting in desperate hope inside Leland Memorial Hospital on the morning of June 19th, 1986 endured the unimaginable. Death comes for everyone but the shock of a sudden death, particularly of someone young and strong, is inconceivable and leaves loved ones suspended in that cruel moment. With the family in our hearts, we continue to focus our attention on the survival of the human spirit when discussing the lessons from Len.

In my mind, I envision his death in the context of the legendary rebirth of the phoenix. Len Bias developed into a beautiful star and burned so bright that his flame engulfed him. However, from that flame, a new phoenix rises. His spirit lives within us, and from that spirit, that image of excellence, we soar toward our dreams.

The raw pain of losing Len created a reservoir of tears I found impossible to regulate, a flood of emotions that would strike me for decades to come. There is a part of me that still idolizes Len Bias and I will always mourn such a bright life and dazzling career cut short. The steel-plated side of my soul took his death as a sign, a lesson towards a safe and healthier lifestyle, and a distant goal that allowed me to put aside my doubts and fears and placed my feet solidly on the road to what would become my life's work.

That might sound a bit much for a sixteen-year-old but my hometown hero, the favorite son of a tight-knit Prince George's County, had suffered the unthinkable. To cope with the crippling grief, I pledged to be like "The Man," my icon of pure grace and strength.

Perhaps teenagers are inherently receptive to transformation since they exist in a continuous state of anticipation, a bundle of potential awaiting the unknown event that will give them direction. Some look for a movement, but no one chooses the tragic loss of an idol as a catalyst. Such a catastrophe happening to a sixteen-year-old forging beyond adolescence produces repercussions for the rest of my life.

1986 marked the onset of my personal rebellion, an individual and internal revolt against despair and disgrace.

As a seven-year-old, I most likely would not have understood Len's passing.

At ten-years-old, I might have mourned for a time and then found a new hero.

As a thirteen-year-old, I would have been torn, asked questions, and wondered about choices.

At twenty-one, I would have had the life skills of an adult to channel my grief.

I was barely sixteen, shyly approaching manhood, questioning my guiding principles on the path to an uncertain future. The magnitude of the tragedy gave me direction. The death of Len Bias was *the* thing in my young life causing me to say *this* is what I am going to do with my life.

Some boys growing into men are stirred to action by an ambition to serve their country; others are driven toward fulfilling childhood fantasies. There are those who meet the girl of their dreams and suddenly, life takes on new meaning. My hometown hero died young and losing someone of such importance and influence changed my way of thinking. Len Bias makes me aware of my purpose, in the way he lived, and the way he died.

Losing Len Bias anchors me at Maryland. He made me proud of being from Maryland and turned the Terps into my basketball team. He lifted us to the height of admiration and his heartbreaking death at his moment of triumph caused the Terrapin Nation more anguish than any outsider can imagine. I decided the only way I could help to alleviate the inner pain and the public mourning was to create a new day by recreating excellence at the University of Maryland.

Len Bias fought his way to College Park from his home in neighboring Landover. If he could do it, so could I. I would follow the path from Temple Hills to Cole Field House and help rebuild the shattered Terrapins.

We adored Len as if he belonged to us and, like when a beloved family member is snatched away, we couldn't move for a while. It was that personal and that painful. For a time, sadness prevailed and there was no soothing balm, no figure of recourse to heal our hearts. In the streets, the newspapers, and on television, Len and Maryland were beaten and bashed to pieces. I kept hoping someone would step up and remind folks of the full measure of "The Man" and all Len had contributed to our community, our pride, and sense of worth. For some, this heartbreak was too much. They abandoned the icon, buried the memories of wonder, and found another hero to follow.

I decided to make a statement by playing basketball for the University of Maryland.

In other words, I decided to be like Len Bias.

Perception is reality anywhere you go, from my home in Stony Creek, Virginia to Timbuktu. My teammate died using cocaine so anyone I meet might believe I use cocaine too. In his or her imagination I'm not just a cocaine user, I'm a "crackhead," the monstrous side of Hollywood's recreational companion, a paralyzing stigma eating at the root of innocence. I have never used cocaine but facts don't matter during a fire. Everybody burns.

"Wow, you are tall. Do you play basketball?"

"Yes."

"What team?"

"Maryland."

"Oh."

After a pitying smirk, they turn away. The matter has been decided and my damnation certain. If they had manners, I'd hear a meaningless "good luck" thrown over a shoulder as they walk away.

During my one remarkable, life-altering season as a teammate of Lenny Bias, a fan would ask about playing in the ACC and urge us to trounce North Carolina and Duke. On June 19, 1986, the shadow of Lenny's death fell over all of us, on the morals of everyone at the University of Maryland, and on the character of his teammates.

Where there had once been joy, we saw distrust in the faces of strangers. Where there had been hope and promise, the eyes that stared at us are filled with "guilt by association" and "birds of a feather flock together." After one season, the three years of athletic combat and proud conquest I'd looked forward to was tarnished and there was nothing in my future but blame and failure.

The state flags lowered to half-staff signified the sentiment of the nation. For me, my freshmen teammates, and the rest of the Terrapin athletic family during the early days following the loss of our brother, the low-flying flags were the ever-present symbols of our new lives filled with shame and suspicion.

In the eyes of the thoughtless, everyone from the University of Maryland shared responsibility for the death of Lenny Bias and for the collapse and disgrace of a renowned tradition. All the student-athletes at College Park were treated like "the usual suspects" but basketball players were "Public Enemy Number One."

Popular opinion carries power, and can be a difficult attitude to modify, so the journey beyond the death of Lenny Bias begins with a battle against an immense crowd of angry and doubtful faces. With depression in command, I slipped into seclusion, each day of solitude is another twenty-four hours smothered by shock. My friend dies, an academic scandal leaves me ineligible for the 1986-87 season, and my world crumbles.

I'm eighteen years old and my life is over.

My sixteen-year-old heart ached as I cried listening to the radio repeat the tragic news the next morning. The only relief was the memory of being in the lay-up line in Cole Field House with "The Man" nearby. So, I stay in the lay-up line and Len is always near, and every morning I wake up feeling that way convinces me to think that way for the rest of my life.

On the day Len Bias died, the courts were empty, the chains strung on the rims silent in the wind. In Temple Hills, no one had the heart to come out and play pickup, to bump and trash talk and fly in the happy madness of basketball. Prince George's County had been inspired by its hometown hero and his death deflated everything.

We suffered the loss of a local superstar, the best basketball player who ever wore Terrapin red. It was unfair and cruel and the disabling pain weaves into the fabric of my life, a hurt I will feel for the rest of my life.

Len was only twenty-two but, as far as I am concerned, he never needed to play another basketball game. He won. He made it and showed me the way. The heartbreak of not having him there to thank, and not having the chance to be his little brother, chisels my youthful purpose and passion into a sustaining core of belief that has ordered and directed my life.

The sorrow, the negative chatter about my Prince George's County community, and the portrayal of the University of Maryland and its student-athletes as the outlaws and criminals of national athletics were flaming arrows shooting at me and my family. To deflect the onslaught, I needed to do right.

In the classroom: Focused.

At home: Focused.

On the court: Focused.

I focused on being Len Bias.

Every day of the excruciating summer of 1986, the nation spoke with a single voice, a mighty chorus of criticism about Maryland and Len Bias. He was a fiend and College Park, in fact, all of Prince George's County, was the swamp that had spawned this monster, and surely the "truth" would be found and all of us punished, whether we'd done anything wrong or not.

The death of Len Bias pounded on the spirit of our community and raged inside my heart, stirring with sorrow and suffering, but, as I've learned, nothing lasts forever and there were signs of renewal. You had to look for them but they were there. On the playgrounds, ball players still argued over the right to be called "Bias" during pickup games. True players recognized the power of that name.

I no longer viewed basketball as a game. I felt a necessity to dominate on the court, to crush competitors, and raise the P.G. County profile back to the pinnacle where Len lifted us. Len Bias passing away at only twenty-two scared me into believing I had to make things better. I had to play basketball for and graduate from the University of Maryland.

For four glorious years, Len Bias uplifted the Terrapin community, reintroduced the University of Maryland to every basketball fan in the nation, and proved the excellence of Maryland Basketball to everyone else. It took one day after his passing to turn College Park and Prince

George's County, Maryland into unwanted outsiders in the academic and athletic world. Len's immortal coach Charles "Lefty" Driesell was replaced and the selection of Robert "Bob" Wade to pick up his mantle proved to be an unpopular decision.

Battered and abandoned, Maryland supporters had to grit their teeth and stiffen their backbones to stand up under an unrelenting flood of rumors, allegations, and outright slander sweeping over their heads like an ocean wave. Everything written or televised about Maryland was front page, lead story, depressing, and painfully personal.

I am P.G. County. I love the Terps. I love Maryland and Maryland needed the Terrapin Nation to come to her rescue. She needed the strength and support of everyone in the county. I thought of myself as a volunteer, someone who could make a difference by doing the right things and by projecting a positive image.

In much the same way that Len used his anger at the ACC as a catalyst to play like a super-human at his "coming out party," I took my frustration and channeled it into inner strength. To deal with the dark portrayal of "The Man," I set out to emulate him at his best and brightest. I played on the courts where he played, shot until dark, carried a ball everywhere I went, and did the things I was told he'd done to polish his craft. In all this I had one objective: Follow Len Bias to the University of Maryland to bring back the joy of basketball for my Maryland.

Chapter 3

THE **AFTERMATH**

"If cocaine could kill Len Bias, no one stands a chance. This clear-cut, unforgettable message eliminates the temptation that misled "The Man" and enables me to focus on the actions that made him great."

TONY

The invasive nature of cocaine reared its head long before its 1986 assault on the campus in College Park, Maryland. To me, cocaine and sports simply do not go together. I couldn't see how one wouldn't automatically close the door on the other. Drugs were a game I knew nothing about. Despite the monumental cultural swing of the cocaine '80s, I failed to make the enticing connection between success, access, and a white powder.

There is no discussion on this topic. When someone tells a cautionary tale of an athlete cut down by drug abuse, no one steps up with a story about how cocaine really helped another athlete reach the top. They don't because those stories don't exist.

Some use, others do not.

The users fail.

End of story.

The transcendent athletes of the 1980s shifted the entire athletic marketplace helping players earn the sort of big money the owners had earned for decades, and making them global commodities with the ability to continue to earn long after their

playing days were over. Trendsetters like Michael Jordan and Vincent "Bo" Jackson used their recognition and status to become major competitors in the corporate world, often more popular than the teams they played on. It was an innovative age with sports marketing gearing up to build superstars and the promotion and coverage of these more-than-human figures may have led to an intoxicating attitude of "I can do anything."

This way of thinking tore through the music world, ripped a hole in Hollywood, and then raged into the rarified air of the super-athlete. The formula was success equals access, and a shooting star like Lenny Bias grew more successful every day of his adult life. Handling success while entering a world of entitlement presented unique challenges because of a sneaky, poisonous combination: privileged stars with a lot of money and liberal attitudes toward cocaine.

Cocaine was everywhere: in hedge funds and movie studios, rock palaces and TV stations, in the boardrooms and on the streets, maybe in Stony Creek, Virginia. The question is whether America really addressed the problem of cocaine use seriously until Lenny Bias proved how deadly it was. History shows that a massive and unforgiving overreaction followed the realization.

At one time, sports-loving boys dreamed of playing for the New York Knicks or the Los Angeles Lakers, wearing a Dallas Cowboys or Pittsburgh Steelers jersey, or becoming a pin-striped Yankee one day. Sports marketing exploded during the 1980s and new revenue streams allowed NCAA conferences to sign big-dollar contracts for the rights to broadcast sporting events, shining a bright light on the student-athletes, modifying their goals, and kids shifted their sights. It was no longer enough to merely play in "The League" or make it to "The Show." You needed to make it with enough spark and fire to grab the brass ring.

The brightness glowing on individual performance makes the amateur more visible than before, providing early incentives and opportunities to live and secure the preferred life, a life with the options their parents never had, magnifying the challenge to maintain their bearings as they matured. Endorsements leading to athletes being worshipped above their sport represented an evolution, part of the natural progression of a capitalist society, with consequences.

Children play for the love of the game. The game grows in popularity through increased exposure, and the game needs to market itself, which catapults young athletes into superstardom. With the spotlight illuminating the athlete, swaying the national focal point toward the individual, the game grows to rely on off-the-field performance to the extent it once relied on wins and losses, amplifying the magnitude of every character flaw. The game changes, and the shortcoming of a sports star dominates the headlines.

By 1986, Lenny Bias had grown larger than college basketball, a rare two-time Conference Player of the Year, and a Maryland legend. Joining a world championship franchise and pulling down the jackpot of a Reebok footwear and apparel contract took the Lenny Bias brand well beyond the sports world. The growth of sports marketing blasted twenty-one and twenty-two-year olds into a world of contracts that could build lasting wealth, and endorsement deals unheard of ten years before, back when these same superstars began to play for the simple love of the game.

The twenty-five million dollar NBA contract and Converse shoe deal signed by "Magic" Johnson along with the lucrative partnership between the Nike Corporation and a youthful Michael Jordan signaled to an attentive generation of ball players a novel and eye-catching equation: basketball success can mean unparalleled financial security. A mirage of wealth would be handed over without any lessons in saving and investment that would keep it from melting away even before the athlete's career was over. The balance of power in the world of sports shifted to favor the star athlete, a creature of trial and error, with the means to try anything, and the chance to fail before the world.

WALT

Len Bias dying from cocaine use overshadows his gift. Everything I knew about the University of Maryland before the summer of 1986 was a glorious celebration of the ascension of local hero Len Bias. When he died, the celebration ended, the crowds vanished, and Maryland Basketball became the scapegoat for a nation. The music faded, the glitter was gone, and all that was left was the constant and unforgiving lights of seemingly endless investigations.

I wanted to bring Maryland back to prominence and be the Len Bias who lived. I understand the fatal mistake Len made. Watching the classic story of an idol's rise and fall has been a powerful message to young and impressionable minds since the first hero. The choice Len made to use cocaine raised a stop sign and clarified the course for me.

I needed to battle every day, hustle until the last shot, and practice until my game matched my desire. The chip on my shoulder from having my idol die and my Maryland slip to become a national laughing stock shaped an intense temperament with an origin too profound to understand at the time.

Losing Len Bias hurt too much.

I'll never lose again, ever.

I entered my junior year of high school during the dreadful summer of 1986 feeling like a machine, brainwashed to work, win, and dominate. The carefree joy of a teenager had been scrubbed away. I had giant footsteps to follow to be the next best from P.G. County so I practiced shooting and dribbling after school every day to be better than the day before. I did not *play* basketball anymore. I *worked* to pursue a calling.

I wanted to be like Len Bias.

Near midnight, November 16, 2004: During what turns out to be my last NBA season, a casual conversation with a Boston Celtics fan shifted my attention to the far-reaching effect Lenny Bias has on American society.

We arrived in Boston late after a game in Philadelphia and

I intended to grab a quick meal at the hotel restaurant before going to bed. A gentleman sitting across from me scanning a menu looked up and asked, "You're Tony Massenburg, right, Len Bias' teammate at Maryland?"

Ahead of my response, he expressed condolences for the loss of a friend, perhaps the only time during my professional career that a stranger mentioned Lenny and followed with an acknowledgement of his teammates' suffering.

I thanked him and we exchanged a prolonged handshake. He removed his eyeglasses and asked, "Do you want to know how the death of Len Bias changed America?" I'd grown used to accounts of what might have been during two stints with the Celtics; I expected a personal interpretation of the gloom that spread over Bostonians at the news of Lenny's sudden death. Instead, the man asked, "Are you familiar with the 'Len Bias law'?"

He proceeded to walk me through a series of events worthy of a John Grisham novel. I was mesmerized and, in the scramble to settle the tab and express my honest thanks for the conversation, I neglected to get his name. The next day, while we gathered for the bus ride to the Fleet Center, a hotel attendant handed me a stuffed manila envelope with the words "Len Bias: Bigger Than Basketball" written on the front. Inside the packet, I found photocopied articles from newspapers, magazines, and legal journals illuminating the mind-boggling claims of the mysterious Celtics fan.

In these articles were the details of how a culture, or sub-culture, within America grew fascinated by cocaine and, in general, regarded it as relatively safe even while research and statistics were nailing down its lethal nature.

Lenny's death caused a legislative firestorm. Events during the six-month period after his death resulted in what is, arguably, the least effective and most reactionary law ever written and passed by Congress. The Anti-Drug Abuse Act of 1986 has been criticized as being written in a rush and approved without sufficient review. Many believe the coverage of a sports superstar's death in the backyard of the White House resulted in legislation being pushed through Congress at an accelerated rate, with unforeseen and disturbing consequences.

The significant and disturbing part of the law is that it created mandatory sentences for drug dealers and drug possession with far longer jail terms for "crack" cocaine—primarily used by blacks—often 100 times as harsh as those for "powder" cocaine—primarily used by whites. The result: thousands of low-level, non-violent drug users, overwhelmingly black and Hispanic, were sentenced to long, irrevocable terms behind bars. By 2002, two million people were incarcerated, five times more than in 1972, and the majority of the people sentenced to prison were black. (*Stanford Law Review*, Dorothy Roberts, April 2004) Former Federal Public Defender and current U.S. Magistrate Judge Michael Nachmanoff called the law a great stain on the federal justice system.

In the summer of 2010, President Barack Obama signed the Fair Sentencing Act into law, the first bill that amended the 1986 Anti-Drug Abuse Act, a law a majority of the nation considered a twenty-four-year travesty. In August of 2013, U.S. Attorney General Eric Holder announced plans to increase prosecutorial discretion, furthering the effort to wipe out the inequalities built into excessively harsh and severe mandatory minimum sentences.

Still, states persist in passing indictments under the so-called "Len Bias law" and, as I discovered reading the details of a 2013 criminal trial in Wisconsin, the disconcerting connection remains a powerfully painful reminder solidifying Lenny as an American legend. Author Michael Weinreb confirmed in a June 2008 piece for ESPN.com that Len Bias' death may be the most socially persuasive moment in modern sport history.

Once again, "The Man" alters my consciousness.

Inside the envelope, along with the illuminating article clippings collected by the Bostonian, I found a handwritten note boldly proclaiming, "JUNE 19, 1986, THE DAY AMERICA DECLARED WAR ON DRUGS." Etched below in small print: "we're losing."

Lenny Bias: my friend, my teammate, my brother.

We know one sure thing: Len teaches us that cocaine is deadly. The lesson hits home and produces aftershocks, loud and lucid, from Prince George's County across the nation. I live wiser with this example. Like riding a bike, I never needed a reminder. Drug use may have been the only opponent capable of stopping Len Bias, and a drug took him down. If cocaine could kill Len Bias, no one stands a chance. This clear-cut, unforgettable message eliminates the temptation that misled "The Man" and enables me to focus on the actions that made him great.

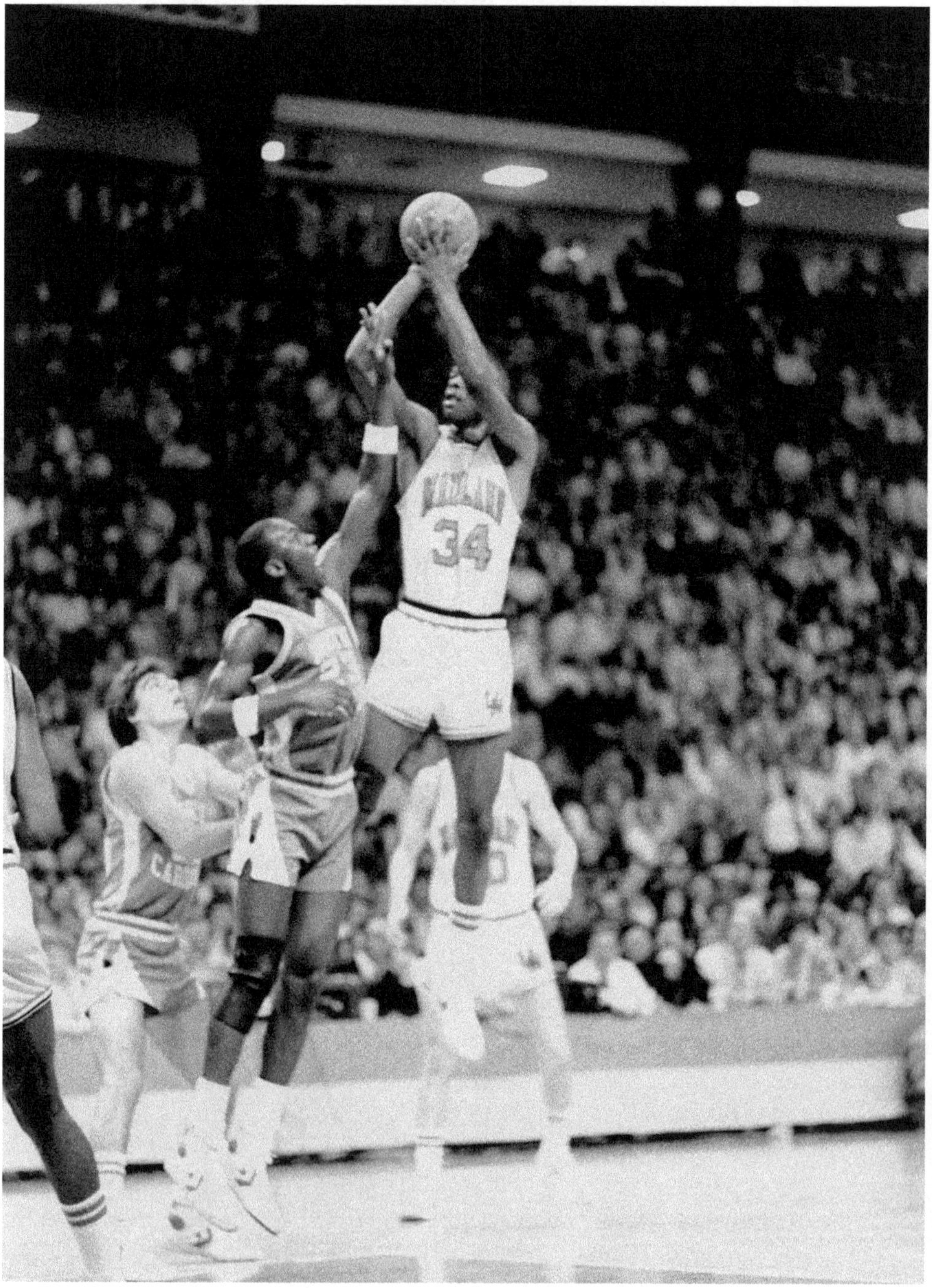

Len Bias rises above Michael Jordan

Chapter 4

TWO ROADS TO **COLLEGE PARK**

"I wanted to be Len."

WALT

Any kid in my Prince George's County neighborhood who supported a college team other than the Georgetown University Hoyas needed a flawless on-court performance to avoid being tongue-lashed. Georgetown Basketball reached deep into the consciousness of suburban DC and much of urban America, inspiring devotion beyond mere sport. The Hoya athletes, the all-out, defiant Georgetown style of basketball, and their complete dominance let me and the world know that a coach who looked like my father and kids who looked like me, with backgrounds like mine, have what it takes to play with conviction, change the game, and succeed at a school previously known for doctors and lawyers.

My family lives in Temple Hills, Maryland but I was born in the District of Columbia and that grants me the right to root for and represent the nation's capital every time I'm involved in a game. Growing up, I watched every Georgetown game I could and bargained to stay up late to see the highlights of any game I missed. Hall of Fame Coach John Thompson, Jr., with his white towel and the smart, warm, tough treatment he gave to his players, was not only a giant in stature but also as respected as any granite monument for his strict rules and winning performance. His teams won.

Georgetown ruled the "DMV," and I proudly sported a Hoya jacket to school and around town, until a cold night in 1983 when my father took me to see a game at the University of Maryland. Watching the Terrapins play from a seat inside Cole Field House altered my life.

Basketball was no longer tiny figures on a TV screen; it was big, loud, and played fast by men moving and crashing at a pace I could never have guessed from the couch.

It was real, live basketball, and I fell in love with the game and "The Man."

TONY

My father, Alvin, nailed a basketball rim to a pole in my grandmother's backyard and suddenly, I had two new friends: The Ball and The Basket. For a six-year-old only child, nothing was more important than these two reliable playmates. It took the standard deep-knee bend, two-hand, underhand launch just to get the ball to touch the net but I would not stop until I could put the ball in the basket just like Dad.

After celebrating my first score, my father picked up the ball and jumped so high that I saw the bottom of his shoes. He slammed the ball through the rim, it bounced off the pole, rolled toward the house like a bowling ball, and I chased after it in amazement. It was the greatest thing I'd ever seen. My Dad could fly! He had to do that again. I ran back with the ball asking him to do it again, and again, and every time we played, I always wanted to see him "dunk it again." I loved the dunk. I added a little jump to my knee bend and underhand toss because I wanted to dunk just like Dad, and my journey began.

My Dad took me with him to the blacktops where they played pickup games and I dribbled on the side waiting for a game to end—that's when the kids ran onto the court to throw up shots until the next game started. After the last game of the day, my

Dad and his buddies would pass me the ball, tell me when to shoot, and give me pointers. They were coaching me, taking me through drills, and I loved every minute of it. I was a ball player like the men I looked up to, a little athlete growing fast.

In the South, football was *the* game and the first sport of the school year, and I couldn't wait to play on a team with my schoolmates. The toughness and aggressiveness I needed to match the gridiron mentality of the kids in Sussex County carried over to the gym class, the backyard, and the basketball courts. Playing organized football at an early age gave me a foundation based on discipline and strength, which are things I can control. On game day, it turned me into a confident kid. Football started the engine that drove the basketball player in me to believe I could. I'm good at something; I can play.

I still couldn't dunk, but my father had a plan.

By the fifth grade, I was only a few inches shorter than my Dad, just big enough to fill in if they needed one more player for the last pickup game of the day. Being on the court with them, on a team with them, made me happier than Christmas morning, but I never scored.

I made baskets all the time on the backboard at the house but my shots banged off the elementary school backboards like bricks. After complaining to my Dad about my shooting woes he told me not to worry, and told me a secret that changed my game.

When my father replaced the rim nailed to a pole with a real fiberglass backboard, he installed it about six inches higher than a regulation basket. Before I could blame him for my poor shooting, he explained that he wanted me to shoot the ball high and be able to jump higher than any of my classmates. He said if I can grab our rim with two hands, the schoolyard baskets would be a cinch, and I'd be flying over my friends. My father knew I wanted to dunk more than anything, and I understood the reasoning behind his method, so I shot high and kept jumping.

Stony Creek Junior High School opened its gymnasium for free play on weekends and my parents allowed me to stay for hours each day. Playing games and hanging with middle school kids helped me learn the ropes and what to expect from teenage life.

On the basketball court, there were three critical questions: Can you touch the backboard? Can you touch the rim? Can you dunk?

Not only could I touch the rim, I could hang from it. That made me special, and I loved the feeling. My first sample of organized basketball came in the seventh grade and it was just in time. My father's strategy had worked. I was flying over my classmates and comfortable shooting at what felt like a low ten-foot rim. By the end of my eighth-grade year, I sprouted from five-feet-eight to six-feet-three and basketball went from a pastime to a passion. I was thrown into the grown-up world of varsity ball the day I walked into high school, a case of "sink or swim," but football and the men in my family made sure I had the experience necessary to rise above the rest. Running faster, jumping higher, rebounding, and blocking shots got me noticed, and it's no coincidence that these are the same skills that kept me in "The League" for thirteen seasons.

Dad had a pretty good plan all those years ago.

Playing varsity from Day One gave me an early introduction to the advanced level of basketball outside of my small rural Virginia town. Hard-fought battles with and against older competitors forced me onto the fast track and lifted me into state-wide competition.

The lessons ranged from subtle to brutal. Some left bruises, others an invaluable understanding of the game, and, together with a homegrown work ethic, my skill set blipped the radar screens at Virginia colleges and universities. I began to believe that basketball could take me beyond the time limit of senior year and the town limit of Stony Creek.

In the summer of 1984, I received an invitation to a basketball camp filled with some of the most talented high school student-athletes in the nation. I could feel the achievement engine of my adolescent brain turn on as I opened the envelope. College coaches from California to Clemson showed up to watch us play and that turned a simple playground game into an opportunity. Suddenly, I was a teenager who could go anywhere and succeed.

I could unlock the door to my future, a door I didn't know existed.

Sherman Dillard, from the University of Maryland, was the first coach from the ACC to approach me during the camp. Coach Dillard, currently an assistant on the Iowa Hawkeyes staff, complimented my performance, said he planned to follow my progress throughout the summer, and looked forward to seeing me have a great senior season when I went back to school. I thanked him with a simple handshake and a smile but the image of Maryland number thirty-four flashed through my mind and, for the first time, I saw a chance to play with the great Lenny Bias.

Stony Creek, Virginia sits in ACC country and kids playing pickup wore mostly Virginia Cavalier or North Carolina Tar Heel gear with a sprinkle of Virginia Polytechnic Institute and State University Hokie (Virginia Tech) here and there. I liked these great teams but this was 1984, a critical year in my development as a player. 1984 belonged to the Maryland Terrapins, and so did I.

When the courtside conversation turned to who would be the "next best," Mike Jordan from North Carolina or local favorite Ralph Sampson of Virginia, I defended the smooth style of Terp number thirty-four. I felt chills listening to the Maryland band lead the crowd in the "Amen Chorus" as Lenny and the Terrapins spanked Duke to win the 1984 ACC Tournament Championship. Knowing Coach Dillard was thinking of me fanned the flames in my heart and the College Park appeal pulled me in.

I needed a Maryland scholarship.

I wanted to play with Lenny Bias.

I wanted to be the next Lenny Bias.

Sharing the thrilling news that the University of Maryland had noticed my skills with Mom and Dad caused my mother to respond with a tried and true piece of down-home wisdom: "Just keep on playing."

I did.

Mom lobbied against placing all my eggs in one red basket,

and my parents may have held a slight preference for in-state Virginia Tech. Both urged me to take my time and research a lot of schools, schedule official visits to the most impressive ones, and be sure I had a feel for each before making a final decision.

I shook hands with dozens of coaches during the summer of 1984, and narrowed my "where to go" wish list to five schools, with the Terrapins ranking number one. Scheduling required visiting Wake Forest and Virginia Tech ahead of Maryland and both schools offered attractive opportunities for me to play right away.

Tyrone "Muggsy" Bogues delivered an excellent sales pitch for Wake Forest and dinner with Wardell "Dell" Curry highlighted an impressive tour of Blacksburg, Virginia, but everything needed to be weighed against the trip to College Park.

Coach Dillard and sophomore Terp Keith Gatlin met us on the steps of the main entrance into Cole Field House for my official visit to the University of Maryland. My parents and head coach "Lefty" Driesell shuffled off to share a meal and Keith took me on a tour of the campus. We walked and talked and realized we were both just country boys. He grew up in Grimesland, North Carolina which didn't sound a whole lot different from Stony Creek, Virginia.

Mostly, we talked basketball. Keith described the makeup of the team and how I would fit in and with every step I took, I hoped to hear him say something about Lenny. Every dormitory he pointed out, I waited for, "and that's Lenny's room."

We crossed a street he called "The Route" to what seemed to be an off-campus housing development and Keith suggested we grab a couple of the other players and hit the "Field House" for a shoot-around. It sounded friendly but I'm sure he wanted to test the Stony Creek skill set that Coaches Dillard and Driesell wanted to add to the Terrapin mix. I wanted to scream "Yes!" but in an attempt to mask my youthful eagerness, I coolly and calmly responded with a straight-faced "OK" like it was no big thing.

We walked into an apartment without knocking and the door closed on Wake Forest, Virginia Tech, and all the other schools.

"The Man" was at home.

Keith introduced me as the new recruit and Lenny responded with a velvet "What's up, Big Young'un?"

"Big Young'un": a fitting term of endearment from teacher to pupil.

The hours rushed by as we played cards, talked trash, told jokes, watched television, grubbed on chips and pretzels, and shot hoops on the outdoor courts with guys I knew would be my future teammates. I had the time of my young life and was sold on College Park. I wanted to play with Lenny Bias and share his life, his basketball brotherhood, his Maryland.

Lenny paid attention to people, even scrawny potential recruits who might just spend a long afternoon and never return. When I returned to campus many months later, "The Man" flashed his million-dollar smile, hit me with an extended high-five, and this time, a resounding, "What's up, Big Young'un?"

The nickname stuck, and so did I.

Coach Driesell, with his charming Southern manners, won over my parents. They liked the small town feel of College Park, and appreciated how close it was to home. Most importantly, Mom and Dad trusted their hearts and trusted my judgment. I had no doubts concerning my love for Maryland and my desire to play ball with Lenny Bias.

When I leaned forward in the car to say we should stop entertaining other offers, my parents agreed. I sat back a Terp and stared out the window at the road between my two homes, daydreaming about winning alongside Lenny.

Two days later, I formally accepted the scholarship to play for the University of Maryland, honored to team up with "The Man."

I thought my decision was right then and I feel even more certain today. Occasionally, a team of very different people will form a close and lasting bond that can only be described as "family." Freshmen fit in, upperclassmen receive fraternal respect, and the captain represents the soul of the unit. Our adoration for Lenny Bias, the incumbent ACC Player of the Year and the finest amateur in the country, neared worship. "The Man" radiated

brilliance in every way and reflections of being his teammate for one season seem to blend with the impossible.

Lenny was more than just a sports hero to a kid from Virginia; he was kind to everyone, the kindness we should all have for one another. It was easy to tell he was raised right. He was a good friend, a teacher, a mentor, and a pillar of constant and unyielding support as I followed him on his way to a second ACC Player of the Year title. But what sticks out is that he just took me in, placed his arm across my shoulders, let me study sheltered under his broad wing, and then pushed me out to demonstrate my own skills free of nagging doubts, shielded from deterrents, and secure in the knowledge that I'd always be a part of the Maryland family.

My Crossland High School team won a return trip to Cole Field House to defend our Maryland State Title only to confront the Northwestern Wildcats and Len's younger brother, Jay. A Bias-led team in Cole Field House is an intimidating challenger and, like so many others, we fell to their divine drive for the championship.

A sprinkling of post-season accolades caused a few colleges to contact me but I heard nothing from the University of Maryland. The Nittany Lions of Pennsylvania State University penned the first letter officially declaring faith in my ability to play at the Division One level. Locally, only American University showed interest in my still-developing skills.

Len Bias raised the curtain on a way to achieve the inconceivable. Consequently, I had a single-minded determination to follow him and this gave me the composure to accept uncertainty and worry while waiting for the must-have letter of affirmation from Coach Bob Wade that would make me a Terp.

Weeks rolled by and, although offers arrived from North Carolina, Wake Forest, and Villanova, College Park seemed uninterested. The true-blue Hall of Fame Coach Dean Smith visited my "hood" and sat in the Crossland High School stands to watch me play. I replied in kind by checking out Chapel Hill. The great Dean Smith, his assistant and current top Tar Heel Roy Williams, and all the players rolled out the baby-blue carpet, and treated me like a king. They went so far as to research my family tree and highlighted a host of relatives living nearby in North Carolina, a tug at my heartstrings.

I went up Philadelphia's Main Line, toured Villanova, and considered the full-court press of College Basketball Hall of Fame Coach Roland "Rollie" Massimino, the architect of the startling 1985 NCAA championship victory over local frontrunner Georgetown.

Coaches Smith and Massimino, proven winners and two of the most respected basketball engineers in the country, wanted me. My confidence skyrocketed, but still no letter from Maryland.

The image of Len Bias was the sole recruiter calling me to College Park but the Terps didn't need anything else. "The Man" was the only incentive I needed. I wanted to be Len, to shine at the University of Maryland, and articulate Maryland pride. While Coaches Smith and Massimino and their staffs will always have a special place in my heart for valuing my effort, nothing was going to pry me out of my Terrapin shell.

My high school coach, Earl Hawkins, worked out a proactive plan to initiate dialogue with College Park. Coach Hawkins reached out, Coach Wade came to Crossland High, and we bonded. Scandal and doubt still swirled around the campus but even with all the adversity and pessimism, none of my family, friends, or mentors screamed, "Do not go to Maryland!" No one talked about a lack of institutional integrity in College Park. The people I trusted applauded my commitment to revitalize the team, the school, and the legend.

Terrapins unite. Maryland is home and family comes first. Without a doubt, my path leads to College Park.

Chapter 5

THE **POWER OF PICKUP**

"The summer before our freshman year, Joe Smith and I put in long hours training with and playing against Walt and Tony, NBA players, guys who had been in our shoes and understood basketball at the highest level. We were learning to be Terps, trying to hold our own against big-time talent, and soaking in the wisdom during our talks about representing Maryland and college life in general. It really helped, especially from a mental standpoint. Our first college game, against Georgetown, we were confident. We were prepared. We had experience."

—Keith Booth, University of Maryland Athletics Hall of Fame, NBA World Champion

TONY

Three weeks after graduating from high school, I drove from Sussex County, Virginia to a new home in College Park, Maryland. An open spot in a small parking lot behind the fabled Cole Field House seemed reserved for my unscheduled arrival. I grabbed the ball I always kept in the back seat and headed straight for the court to fulfill a fantasy: a vertical leap to a two-handed slam for Basket Number One of my Terrapin career.

Longtime fans of college basketball can recount the memorable contests and events that made Cole Field House a legend. Watching on television as Lenny dominated both ends of the

"Field House" reminded my parents of the landmark 1966 Texas Western versus Kentucky National Championship game. They tell me that game, the first time an all-black starting five won the NCAA title by defeating Adolph Rupp's slow-to-embrace-integration attitude and game plan, was the most important sporting event in the battle for civil rights in America. I looked around to imagine what that period of time must have felt like and realized it happened right where I was standing.

History.

An awesome sensation rings down to my toes when Dave Dickerson opens the locker room door and we exchange high-fives for the first time. I slept in the locker room the first night—or it could have been in heaven—I'm not sure there's a difference. The next morning, while exploring the different levels of Cole, a door opened to a hidden gem, a cozy auxiliary gymnasium. During the summer break, when youth camps and conventions occupy the main court, the hidden secret at the heart of Maryland Basketball is nurtured inside the intimate "Small Gym."

At noon on day two, most of my new teammates, a few Maryland football players, and a collection of scholarship student-athletes from other DC area colleges mixed it up with street legends and rising superstars in a three-hour prizefight. The term "Pickup Basketball" doesn't even begin to give you the full flavor of these games, and Lenny had yet to show up.

Six hours later, we meet again to tango with a mix of special guests and NBA players including Terp great John Lucas and All-Star Washington Bullet Jeff Ruland, invited by Coach Driesell as a treat for his basketball camp kids. Being immersed in upper echelon basketball for the first forty-eight hours of College Park life makes an indelible physical and psychological impression, and I see this, correctly, as the way I'm going to spend the next four years. This is the proven-effective Terrapin Way: blending the cream of the crop together in a wild, endless dance that brings out all the joy of basketball competition. It takes me back to the playground and rainy weekends in the junior high school gym, pure athletics, and it fires a rush of excitement across every nerve in my body.

Choosing Maryland feels right.

A star-studded cast returns to the "Small Gym" the following day and the panorama resembles a "Twilight Zone" episode with superb ball players masquerading as everyday people looking for the best place to "get it in," slang for high-intensity basketball. The level of talent far surpasses my amateurish expectation. Even on the high-caliber basketball circuit I traveled to get to College Park, I'd never seen or played in games like this.

Big men handling the ball like a yo-yo and point guards finishing at the rim with forty-inch vertical leaps confirm my theory that basketball is the athletic backbone and soul of the DC region. The All-World performance of Lenny Bias elevates the sport in the region and the advantage the locals gain from years of studying and scrimmaging with "The Man" is ratified in the off-season marathons in College Park. It's a prerequisite, an informal freshman ballplayer orientation with a revolving door of exceptional athletes bringing super competition, and an almost mystical energy to Maryland Basketball. Four months before Coach Driesell's innovative "Midnight Madness," I was playing in a daily midday mayhem in College Park where an unmatched standard of athletic excellence was cultivated one phenomenal pickup game at a time.

The moment I've been anticipating since the tenth grade, my first pickup game with Lenny, exceeds all expectations and becomes one of the most precious memories of my life. Dave Dickerson and I were so excited about basketball and being Terps that we lived in the team locker room for the first few days and while suiting up to play one-on-one, "The Man" walks in with my freshman classmate Greg Nared and rising senior Jeff Baxter.

We exchange Terrapin pleasantries and Lenny asks if we want to roll with them into the city to hoop with the DC elite. I would have walked all the way to Washington to play in that game. We pile five deep into a tank-like Oldsmobile, the jewel Lenny called his "limo," pep rallying all the way to American University, raring to explode from the parking lot. Prior to unlocking the car doors to turn us loose, Lenny swivels to face us, gets our undivided attention, and melodically declares, "We are Maryland," in a way eerily similar to the modern-day chant.

I enter the gymnasium last and hear someone shout, "I got Bias." I'm new, a freshman, and ready to accept playing with whoever picks me up. I'll always remember the next moment as one of the last pure joys of my boyhood, a once-in-a-lifetime experience. Lenny announces that he's going to sit out until the next game so the five of us can play together. My idol, Lenny Bias, wants to team with me. I am seventeen, a Terrapin, and I'm going to be playing alongside "The Man."

Thinking back to that time still gives me the chills. After a quarter-century of world-class championship basketball, I remember a pickup game with nothing on the line, and no strategy except play to the top of your ability to make "The Man" proud.

The fierce competition at American University verifies the existence of a powerful basketball society and Lenny rises head and shoulders above them all. "The Man" put on a two-hour show. I played my role: Sidekick, fortunate just to be there. We won every game as Lenny unleashed his full repertoire: jumpers, hooks, rebounds, game-winners, everything. I watched more than I contributed.

The final shot will stay with me forever. Lenny took down a rebound in traffic, with three players draped on him, and went right back up. When I say, "right back up," I mean I don't think he even bent his knees. He just shot right back up, and reverse-dunked without even looking. No pump fake, no side moves, just power and grace. Dave Dickerson and I looked at each other in complete disbelief. Not only didn't we believe that Lenny could make a shot like that, we didn't think there was a player in the United States who could do it.

Stay tuned, Lenny will repeat this move later in a game when it really counted.

Afterwards, we huddled to share congratulations on accomplishing the Terrapin mission and walked out together, just the

way we walked in. Halfway to the car, Lenny swings his arm around my neck, as he often did during our year together, and says, "Represent Maryland wherever you go. Make them remember that you're a Terp."

The triumphant stroll and brief chat with "The Man" stirs my teenage soul. I belong. I'm the teammate of the best basketball player in the country, Lenny Bias. Wherever the road leads, forever, I'm among a special group of men: College Teammates of the Awesome Lenny Bias.

WALT

The outdoor baskets on the South Hill side of the College Park campus received high honors for hosting top talent. The "Asphalt Square Garden," a perfectly placed court surrounded by dormitories filled with scholarship student-athletes, prompted visitors to pray their day "hooping" at Maryland includes an appearance by "The Man" arising from his suite to bless the crowd with blacktop virtuosity. I began praying as soon as my parents gave me the OK to tag along with my sister, Stephanie, on a visit to College Park. My father led me to the South Hill courts before escorting my sister to her destination and I dribbled into a life-altering occasion.

One of the kids shooting hoops spots me and yells, "We got ten. Shoot for teams." While kneeling to tighten my laces, I notice a door swing open, and through the shadows of a sun-splashed tree Len Bias and Keith Gatlin emerge from Washington Hall like soldiers on parade. Without breaking stride, the dynamic duo politely asked for permission to play and before the two guys preparing to pick teams managed to pick their chins off the asphalt, each superhero pointed at four of us earthlings and turned us into spellbound ball boys. My first time playing on the College Park campus, I am a teammate of Len Bias. The smile painting my fourteen-year-old face resurfaces whenever I reflect on the impact of the inspirational moment.

Len swished the first shot and the ball splashing through the chain net made a perfect sound I hear whenever I think of that day. I tried to be perfect, to make all the right moves, and I assisted on Len's game-winner which set up a most memorable high-five as he dashed away with Gatlin chasing. A kid asked, "Are you a recruit?" and before saying "no," I think "yes," and the goal to be like Len is reinforced. One pickup game with "The Man" takes me to a new height from which I've never descended.

Returning to College Park as a scholarship player ready to run with the best and finding that the team prefers playing pickup on the South Hill courts tells me they choose competition over comfort. The "DMV" shooters, scrappers, dunkers, thugs, and choirboys coming together to "put in work" didn't need Cole Field House. The shade-less courts of scorching and cracked asphalt had a storied history of must-see action and the street ball brand of competitiveness players craved not so long ago. I should fit right in.

The example of excellence Lenny Bias sets by dominating the summer games of 1985 redirects the superiority compass so that it points north to the University of Maryland, and anyone seeking high-level basketball followed the crowds to College Park. The most confident "hoopsters" in the region camped in our little corner of basketball paradise along with a diverse collection of onlookers and up-and-comers wanting to sample and appreciate the power of the Terrapin Way: Get Better or Get Off the Court.

There is no doubt in my mind that Maryland was the perfect place for a freshman ball player to learn the ropes. Pickup was the single constant. From Cole Field House to Leonardtown to South Hill, basketballs bounced on campus courts from breakfast until dawn. An early-morning shooting contest with Lenny turned into a quick game of one-on-one and then Keith Gatlin yells for John Johnson to hurry. Five minutes into the two-on-two, future NFL players Ferrell Edmunds and Warren Powers jump in and ignite the play with a preference for physical hoopla, provoking a spirited aggression required to match their fancy for combat.

A crowd gathers, we have enough for full-court games and

another must-see event unfolds. At random intervals, new clusters of contestants join the basketball bash in a constant flow, adding fresh sets of skills to the potent jambalaya of talent, making anytime the right time for ultra-competition.

It became a local legend. Pickup games on campus at Maryland provide the ultimate basketball challenge. The aura of success Lenny Bias creates at Maryland transforms every court and hoop in College Park into a basketball temple for the whole "DMV" with area "hoopsters" eager for the pilgrimage. We hopped from our dormitories to the eminent proving ground, every day.

Advantage: Terps.

Of course, the "Gridiron Gangsters" from Maryland Football tried to intimidate and dominate, pushing and daring the mix of ready-for-action athletes from the South Hill community to shove back. Without striped shirts and whistles, you either learned to hold your own or were blown off the courts. Bragging rights won before morning classes might be revoked over lunch with word of your humiliation circulating throughout "The Quad" before the afternoon games on the Leonardtown courts across Route One.

Days of inclement weather required synchronizing with the track and field guys and the football players on a time and place to play indoors, and the best of the rest followed the grapevine. Cole Field House always ranked as the crowd's favorite court, either the main floor or the "Small Gym," but discovering that a prototypical gymnasium existed, hidden inside the Health and Human Performance building that opens for free play at noon, changes the game. "North Gym" was the unanimously preferred basketball Mecca when the DC summer heat reached its unbearable humid norm. It was only a fifteen-minute speed-walk from the "The Quad" if a volunteer couldn't be found to drive and feed quarters to the meter.

Once inside, the seventy-two-degree air, a luxury not found inside Cole Field House, makes any sacrifice worth the effort. Two full courts of pristine hardwood floors and classic wooden backboards drew the super-talented like a super-magnet and "North Gym" turns into a daily destination where basketball

players measure up against the best, a time-tested method of improvement.

For Terrapins, the lessons remain invaluable.

From our first conversations, I desperately wanted to hear personal stories and anecdotes from the men who played alongside Len Bias. I still felt grief, so I knew they were still in pain. Instead of digging, I remembered his highlights, and the excitement and great fortune of teaming with Bias for that single all-too-short afternoon. It was a turning point that elevated my confidence and I arrived on the Maryland campus an elite teen and unflappable streetball player, ripe for the legendary pickup battles of College Park.

Washington Hall faced the action, the blacktop ballet, and I stepped out of my dormitory suite directly onto the court thinking about Len and the way it felt running with him, and how he played to win even though he was playing with a bunch of youngsters. He ran off the court a champion. That's how I wanted to feel every day, after every game.

We expected opponents to exert maximum effort going against a Terp, attempting to capitalize on the slightest mistake and make a commanding statement. Therefore, we upheld an unwritten campus-wide rule:

The only messages delivered on our university grounds would come from Terrapins: Dominate and defend turf.

Winning your game and staying on the court to face the next challengers meant everything. Unless a Terp contributes to the victory, visitors to campus, in particular ball players from other universities, ought to leave College Park as losers and wiser for the lesson. If an NBA guy performs well and walks away victorious, we rolled back to our rooms crediting his experience, and going over every small detail of his play. After all, the man plays professional basketball. On the rare occasion of an unknown player receiving that fleeting fifteen minutes of glory, we recognized it as a cosmic glitch and set out to restore Terrapin authority. It was an urban dissemination of physical education not replicable in the confines of a Terrapin team practice.

Sparked by the elemental need to prevail, the atmosphere around "The Quad" shifted from tranquil to thunderous during the pickup games. Win, walk off the court a certified champion, and you spend the remainder of the day under the rainbow of success. Losing ruins every hour you must wait until the sweet opportunity for vengeance comes around again.

The NBA players set the tempo. Their expertise and a motivational presence excited a pack of challengers ranging from veterans on overseas teams to streetwise "hoopers" with unproven skills. Most of the unknowns shot on the side courts for more than an hour, trying to assemble a team that can win, watching four, five, maybe six games start and end for one life-changing chance to show and tell.

The University of Maryland became the regional headquarters of basketball achievement, a beautiful athletic chemistry, and this winning formula produced such incomparable summertime competition that NBA players likened it to pre-season training camp scrimmages. This potent mixture kept them coming back to College Park and adding their explosive talents to those of the best of the current Terrapins. This combination pushed everyone on the court to play at their limit every possession or pay the price.

The resulting "Be Triumphant" culture permeates Terrapin life and was a primary factor in our resurrection as a nationally-respected institution. Internalizing the elevated expectations of summer gives us wings to fly on the rarified air of well-founded self-assurance from "North Gym" into the regular season to face our ultra-talented NCAA foes. We became refined products of our enlightening environment. Maryland basketball players never experienced a drop-off in talent and competitiveness between seasons. The Terrapin revival required year-round dedication and we welcomed the summer schooling.

Losing a dear brother and our place in history reinforces the "me against the world" reaction common among athletes fighting tough odds. Victory in a time of tragedy feels impossible, but winning is marvelous therapy, and no one needed to win more than

a Maryland basketball player. If we laughed, received a word of encouragement from a pro, found a penny, or felt like crying only once in a day, we counted it as a huge victory in the healing process. We jumped back onto the courts agitated by detractors and a "you will see, we can" attitude shapes into a Terrapin Basketball resolution. Driven by the will to survive, a passionate motive to affect perception, and a "watch how we come back next year" mindset, we played pickup games filled with anger at the cruelty of life and a determination to triumph over loss. We needed to win, and each summer our compelling philosophical foundation spreads through the basketball program and into the University forming an underground platform for resurgence.

In time, Lenny's proclamation that "We are Maryland" emerges as a proud statement of fact, a shout-out to the world that we knew exactly who we were, we were not defeated, and we would never give up.

During the transition between Coaches Wade and Williams, I counted on one constant: great pickup games always happening somewhere on campus. The chaos of a leadership change pushed me toward becoming a super-sophomore and the steady presence of Tony Massenburg, our senior captain, along with NBA World Champion Adrian Branch, provides the veteran challenge and requisite homework to encourage a proper understanding of climbing the Terrapin Way. After all, they learned the Maryland Way with "The Man." Training with Massenburg and Branch gave me a direct connection to Len Bias and each small step of success in the battle against basketball royals bolstered self-confidence and made the October transition to NCAA competition only another challenge to overcome and not an insurmountable roadblock to my future.

The honor falls on me to preside over the summer sessions in 1993, and the heartfelt obligation to reflect the lessons we learned from Len Bias dictates my daily course of action. It was my responsibility to be certain that Terrapins realize the mammoth distinction between the NBA and the NCAA, and dangle the golden carrot of the future in front of anyone in view.

I intended to dominate every game, to move past my limits, and win. Winning sharpens my craft and presents an image of Terrapin leadership that gives Johnny Rhodes, Joe Smith, or John Doe a template to build in the way top Terp Keith Gatlin showed me how to manage a game and my adult life. With the legends, "League Men" Branch and Massenburg, and Jerrod Mustaf, a first-round draft pick after two years starring for the Terps, sustaining the driving momentum and furthering the custom of coming home to train in College Park, providing the priceless, career-shaping chance to tussle with the best in the NBA, we lived by the adage, "Get Better or Get Off the Court." We chose to get better as did Duane Simpkins, Keith Booth, and the young Terrapins who received unparalleled feedback as they exercised the privilege of measuring themselves daily against first-class professional athletes.

The Terrapin Way stands as a time-tested and league-verified recipe for success. Compete against the elite and you will improve or disappear. Once the convention of celebrated pickup basketball took over "North Gym," the competition shot to an all-time high and made "North at Noon" the one and only place to play.

Cole Field House fit the formal. "North Gym" belonged to the blue collar. The air conditioning was long gone and an oppressive heat, both in degrees and aggression, deterred the timid while the NBA players cherished the sweatbox atmosphere. Of course, wherever the pros choose to play, the best of pickup ball players follow. The convergence of NBA stars, continental players, college kids, and conspicuous sports agents in College Park for Afternoon Delight creates a charmed opportunity for Terrapins who understood the great fortune of being able to learn, build, and grow without leaving their backyard. Lines formed for "North Gym 101," a phenomenon complete with tactical lessons in life that would prove applicable each November on the long road to "The Big Dance."

Shooting drills and intra-squad pickup games certainly help, and camaraderie absolutely increases team chemistry, but the real lesson of the "North Gym" experience was the quest to push beyond your limits or face daily beat-downs by better players—the best possible learning environment for basketball potential.

The "North Gym" experience sends Terrapins back to their dormitories to think of ways to outwit the best, a powerful analytical process yielding fantastic physical results. "North Gym" forces the scholarship-athlete to survive in the exacting, must-win world of professional basketball. Learn to claim victory with each possession: A lesson for life.

"North Gym" scrimmages were played with the energy and flow of an NBA playoff game against a familiar foe. The first crew to score seven holds court. Every made basket, from the monster dunk to the deepest jump shot, equals one point, and each contest feels like an audition designed to expose every weakness. A loss results in a demoralizing hour-long wait for another try on the main court, hence the tension on the floor and the heckling of the boisterous sideliners. This rough and tumble mentality creates a training ground where baby Terps learn to live up to a level of brutal competitiveness they'd never experience in a real NCAA game. The Terrapins enjoyed a luxury that increased in value throughout their college careers and beyond, simply walking across campus to join twenty professional basketball players in top-flight competition and timely conversation on proficiency in athletics.

College Park basketball offered basic instructions for developing winners: commit to "North Gym 101" and follow the directions—easy math. A constantly changing collection of gifted older men groomed young Terrapins to prevail and the kids who subscribed to the "North Gym" mission and mindset recognized the chance as extraordinary, keenly absorbing the fruits of summers filled with superior competition.

It might be true on most courts and campuses across the nation that a Division One basketball player can feel calm and confident as he steps onto his summer court of choice, certain that he's the top player on the floor. That sure wasn't the case at Maryland during my tenure as a Professor of Pickup. Not ever.

Gracious but unforgiving professionals regulated "North Gym," educating student-athletes in areas of advanced study where the college scholarship falls short. The constant uphill battle to score, defend, and win in every game, every day, every play steels the green Terrapins with a pressurized weapon of confidence that takes the NCAA by storm.

With Evers Burns joining Walt, Jerrod Mustaf, and me in the NBA, the university program that the media ruled dead sends four Terps to "The League" within a three-year span and the summer games on the Maryland campus continued to rival the best basketball in the country. Even though it was no longer climate-controlled, "North Gym" retained its rank as a basketball nerve center, with industrial fans at each exit circulating hot air. The "ballers" endured the stifling humidity and sweat for the assurance of consistent, high-octane competition, and the prospect of taking part in the performance art festival on the main court inside that old gymnasium with its classic hardwood and wooden backboards. I suppose that nicer places to play existed: cooler, newer, more centrally located, easier to access, with free parking, and a locker room, even a trainer nearby in case of an emergency.

There might have been nicer places to play but they weren't the hot, hardwood hall where veterans held court, and local legends were punished for overconfidence. There was only one place for true players and in "North Gym," the best taught the rest the meaning of winning.

A cast of regulars and special guests convened at high noon, five days a week, three hours a day from May through October when the college players assembled for team practice and the pros shipped off to training camp. On the far court, at least six of the ten contenders carried NBA credentials. The other four promising ballplayers might be Terrapins Johnny Rhodes, Joe Smith, and Keith Booth along with a Euro-Basket star known only as "Valentine."

Cordial small talk ends as the opening pass signals the onset of the all-important battle to establish court supremacy. The first victory of the day is a championship, making the second game a title defense, and three wins in a row equals a blatant dynasty. Meanwhile, the side court games and sideline politics prepared the next challengers.

The "must-win" atmosphere grew from South Hill to "North Gym" and emerged as world-class basketball, always within walking distance for Terps. Through my fifteen years of training and

playing summer pickup games from sea to sea, the spectacular and strong-willed brand of basketball generated by the jamboree we termed "North Gym 101" still ranks second to none. The top-notch competitiveness stemmed from deep roots in the culture of the Washington, DC region and saturated the backbone of Maryland Basketball. The Terrapin shell regenerates, nourishing the foundation for our remarkable renaissance in clear view for those willing to look.

A day playing with or trying to defeat a member of the National Basketball Association changes the game for a student-athlete. Consider Terrapins Evers Burns, Joe Smith, and Obinna Ekezie getting intensive on-the-job training under the attentive, if not gentle, care of Tony Massenburg along with such NBA royalty as All-Star Chris Webber and Defensive Player of the Year Marcus Camby, molding them from neophytes into players fit for the under-the-basket warfare of "The League."

At the same time, Terp swingman Laron Profit chases sharpshooter Chris Whitney through a man-mountain of screens, and learns to score against lockdown defensive specialist Bruce Bowen and somehow prevent super guard Stephon Marbury from creating another highlight.

An exceptional drive to win is born and nurtured in College Park. Burns, Smith, Ekezie, and Profit achieve their NBA dreams and the Terps rebound from merely tournament-worthy to regular participants in the "Big Dance" and evolve into a leading national program. In "North Gym," the lessons continue. Profit, now a top Terp, NBA assist champion Rod Strickland, and local stars and future NBA players David Vanterpool and Roger Mason, Jr. challenged standout Terrapin Steve Francis, who in turn inspired apprentice Juan Dixon and recruit Steve Blake. A wave of confidence grew, and with Massenburg bringing the old school to Chris Wilcox and Lonny Baxter, Coach Williams led Maryland to consecutive Final Four appearances and, in 2002, a National Championship done the Terrapin Way.

All this a tradition and a legacy left to us by Len Bias.

Chapter 6

MOVING ON WITH **BOB WADE**

Legendary Maryland coach "Lefty" Driesell resigns in the fall of 1986.

Maryland hires Bob Wade to resurrect a damaged squad.

TONY

Like every kid I ever played ball with, I wanted to be a professional basketball player, although my drive might have been a bit stronger than most. My mother still has a specially-made notebook with every report card I've ever received. There was an extra page each year with a few questions, one of which was "What Do You Want to Do When You Grow Up?" From second grade on, I wrote the same answer: "Play Pro Basketball."

All those years, long after I declared my intention to play pro ball (a real long shot for a kid from Stony Creek), the posters on my bedroom wall seemed to come alive every night and I'd watch Julius Erving flying above the rim in the vintage Virginia Squires uniform he wore before I knew him as "The Doctor." I dozed off thinking of basketball, hoping my last vision of the day ignited a fantastic dream of playing in a roundball wonderland, practicing a kid's version of child psychology.

Naïve and anxious but knowing I was on the road to the goal of a lifetime, I stepped onto the College Park campus with great

expectations, set to learn the game alongside the best player in college basketball. As advertised, Lenny displayed an All-American skill set and I recognized the enormous challenge I faced to get even close to his level of proficiency. Every practice during the 1985-1986 season, I battled with the most talented player in America and fantasized about guarding him on a Sunday afternoon in the NBA Game of the Week. Lenny was certain to make it and the desire to join him there grew stronger every day. The incredible possibility of being drafted by the Celtics in three years to receive a top-flight internship with Lenny and a Hall of Fame frontcourt offered a potent incentive to match the phenomenal "Bias-to-Boston" triumph.

The crushing defeat and terrible loss as Lenny reached "The League" and never played was the cruel spur that kept me going in an endless drive to run the extra mile, do the extra set of squats, shoot another dozen foul shots, always working to be ready wherever the journey leads.

After spinning through time in painful limbo, the shock of losing Lenny eventually eased enough for me to enter recovery mode and begin to piece together a way forward, but the indescribable quake and collapse of my young world still lingers. Those minutes inside the waiting room of Leland Memorial Hospital ending with the horrifying news of my friend's unimaginable death remain the worst moments of my life.

The stunning revelation of cocaine intoxication turns heartbroken teammates into public villains, and a black cloud of controversy smears our reputations at the time we were scuffling just to defend against a tidal wave of grief. When sportswriter and current ESPN personality Jackie MacMullan said that we would pay for staying with Maryland, we had no idea of the cost. I believe, without reservation, Coach Driesell wanted to stand with us and guide his group of broken young men through the nightmare loss of our brother, but darkness and suspicion intervened. An inquisition leads to courtroom proceedings and soon thereafter, Charles "Lefty" Driesell resigned as our head coach. With no one to turn to and everyone looking, we suffered alone.

Given the bleakness of our situation and the doubts about our future, finding a coach willing to lead our beleaguered program seemed impossible. The unpredictable and volatile atmosphere on a campus where everyone lived under suspicion certainly didn't help the search for the right candidate.

For a sorrowful team of teenagers drowning in the wake of terrible misfortune, the selection of a replacement for Coach Driesell did not register as a possibility, much less a priority. We were dealing with nerve-racking rumors that the entire 1986-1987 basketball season might be canceled. A new head man for a lifeless team didn't seem all that important. We were more worried about our scholarships being withdrawn and seeing all our dreams come crashing down.

In 1986, choosing Coach Bob Wade as the man to steer Terrapin Basketball through the storm added more pressure to our already-stressed existence. He was a legend as a high school coach but remember this was 1986 and it wasn't an accident that the ACC, dominated by schools from the South, had never seen a head basketball coach who was black. Fair or not, there was considerable criticism about bringing in a black coach whose success came at the high school level. As a team, we were already struggling, and both the condemnation and the feeling of needing to support our new coach were burdens the players simply didn't need. There was no expectation of success for the battered Maryland team, just a chorus of "I told you so" waiting for failure to fall on us.

The normal academic and social challenges freshmen experience were magnified. Reporters seeking a juicy story would pop up out of nowhere with cameras and microphones, and some unscrupulous members of the press even tried to pose as students to get the scoop on the worst times of our lives.

Coach Wade might have been the right man to hire following the tragedy and the fallout, but he would have had to walk on water to succeed (and even then, some would have yelled, "Look, Wade can't swim!")

I believe now as I did then: Coach Wade accepted the

challenge to lead a lost crew because, like all of us, he wanted a better University of Maryland. The hot lights of intense scrutiny exposed every tiny fault and, arguably, left Coach Wade too busy defending himself to take sufficient care of a group of badly battered young men.

Being suspended for an academic infraction that I was powerless to dispute and barred from practicing with my teammates nearly destroyed my will to chase the dream at Maryland but the path remained clear. Enduring the loss, the defamation, the suspension, and the adjustment from being "Lefty" Driesell's recruit to being Bob Wade's inherited player trying to pick up the pieces would make me the strongest teenager in the country even if it didn't create the best environment to wake up to each day. I couldn't let the circumstances beat me. I just had to survive during the nightmare.

When the team bus pulled away from Cole Field House on its way to face North Caroline State in the first away game of the 1986-87 season, I was left behind. I was hurt and angry with constant reminders of two devastating losses everywhere I turned. I funneled the anger into willpower and the absolute determination it took to push past the cruelest moments of my life pours into everything I become. My only solace was remembering Lenny, feeling him speaking in my heart and lifting me over the stumbling blocks.

I set the good times with Lenny on a continuous loop in my head to fight missing him and to inspire me to be just like him. I thought back to my first bus ride to a Terp road game, an intra-squad scrimmage in Salisbury, Maryland, and remembered feeling the anxiety run down my spine as we crossed the Chesapeake Bay Bridge because I would have to guard "The Man."

Lenny led us into the packed gymnasium to a standing ovation. He waved to the crowd, stretched across the reserved section of bleachers, and started clapping with the fans for the teams playing the Salisbury intra-squad scrimmage. They loved him. I saw it in the way their faces lit up. Lenny was a quiet superstar with a heart of gold, but competition turned him into a dominator and it didn't matter if it was a scrimmage or the finals, he played to win, and I had to guard him. I spent the two-hour bus ride back to College Park licking my wounds, armed with an unmistakable appreciation for why he's called "The Man."

I fought isolation for a year, doing three workouts a day mixed with a three-hour study session and Lenny constantly on my mind and in my ear. When my legs burned and I wanted to stop, I'd think of Lenny doing squats so he could levitate the way I saw him rise over six-feet-eleven defensive stopper and future four-time NBA champion John Salley from the Georgia Institute of Technology. Lenny said he could take two dribbles and pull up from anywhere even if Salley knew he was going to shoot. With that confidence, a great work ethic turned skill into success. That's why he stayed in the weight room. That's why I stayed there as well.

On the days the team traveled for away games, I lifted weights early and then listened to the game on the radio from the "Small Gym" inside Cole Field House, shooting, rebounding, running the floor and sliding as if I was in the game until the final buzzer, and every loss of that winless ACC season burned because I knew, and the team knew, I could have helped us beat those squads. My brothers from the "Lefty" era, Derrick Lewis, John Johnson, Greg Nared, Dave Dickerson, and Phil Nevin; the toughest nineteen and twenty-year-olds I've ever known, formed the core of the 1986-1987 team that bore the burden of rebuilding a world missing its brightest star. I love the '86-'87 team and I hope the Terrapin family and fans of fortitude appreciate them for holding on to the dream and proudly wearing their uniforms at that most difficult time. From the trauma to the public condemnation, they overcame more than any team in the country, and because they did not give up, I had a chance, and that's all my restless spirit needed.

I couldn't play or practice with my teammates but there was always the Maryland Secret: pickup basketball. The difference was that, instead of playing against tall and gangly basketball players, I was out mixing it up with the 300-pound bruisers of the Maryland Football team, guys like NFL-bound O'Brien Alston, Ben Jefferson, Ferrell Edmunds, and Warren Powers.

I'd always been an old school physical ballplayer but the combination of all the time in the weight room and smashing under the basket with the "Gridiron Gangsters" meant that I came out of the spring semester with twenty more pounds of muscle, another inch in height, and a whole new attitude.

Summer, 1987: my first time playing organized basketball since March of 1986 finally came in the Kenner League at Georgetown, an intensely competitive tradition in the "DMV." I made sure to get to the gym early, not for the extra time to warm up but to be the first in line to grab a jersey. If possible, I wanted to wear Lenny's number thirty-four. I needed it to go along with my deeply felt responsibility to "The Man" and the legend. Fate stepped in: thirty-four was the first jersey I pulled out of the bag. Twelve to fifteen jerseys crumpled together in a bag, and I snag thirty-four on the first grab. How did that happen? It had to be.

It was a good summer. In the same way Dad's six-inch higher rim made me jump, all that time shoving around linemen and running backs made basketball players feel like rag dolls, and I was moving people all over the place. I'd arrived at Maryland an adequate teenage player but now I was a twenty-year-old man and my whole style of play changed. If you couldn't physically match up with me, I was going to use my strength to dominate, and from that summer on, that was the way I played, both at Maryland and throughout my pro career. Future Hall of Fame defender Dikembe Mutombo, first-round draft pick John Turner and I tore up the league. My team won the championship, and like every winning moment on the basketball court, I thought of Lenny and our run at the 1986 title.

We entered the '86 NCAA Tournament brimming with confidence, intent on winning the national championship, believing all basketball things were possible with Lenny Bias at our side. Lenny dominated his last college game, the last game we played together, scoring thirty-one points with twelve rebounds against the University of Nevada, Las Vegas (UNLV). We fought hard but failed to provide the support Lenny needed to outlast the Running Rebels, and the first magical ride of my young life ends too fast. Like the final performance of a superstar on tour, the last show closes bittersweet.

Falling short of the title stung but knowing those were the final moments I would play with "The Man" felt like a sword thrust in comparison. Crying, sad, and upset, we rallied around Lenny and followed his lead, finding comfort by focusing on our collective bright future. Huddling for what would be our last time together as a unit, I listened to Coach Driesell sum up our accomplishments and put a bow on the season, and I watched Lenny. Thirty-one points, twelve rebounds, Player of the Year, NBA-bound. I wanted to be him.

Lenny was my guiding star to the next level. His presence and dominance were the most powerful elements in my world. By the time my draft day arrives, "The Man" would have been a three-year veteran and possibly an All-Star and World Champion, and that would have meant three summers of Lenny coming back to campus and schooling us "young'uns" on how to succeed with and against the best players in the world. Counting on determination and the lessons from Lenny, I planned to work my way into "The League," not for an endorsement or to satisfy a youthful wish to play on a favorite team, but to join "The Man."

Exiting the Long Beach Arena following the UNLV game, I acted on an impulse and thanked Lenny for everything, for being our leader and my brother. He responded with a passionate directive: "Take care of my Maryland."

The words gripped my heart. I felt love, the love of Maryland, of teammates, of family, and desperation for more time with "The Man," another game, another practice. Missing him already, fighting tears, I promised to meet him in the League in three years. Smiling, Lenny followed custom, threw his arm around me, tucked me under his wing, and said, "Make it happen."

The impact of his arm rests heavy on my shoulders, and it supports me. It's my inspiration.

I could feel Lenny smiling down on me as I put on my Maryland

jersey for the first time since that last game with "The Man," all those months ago, proud that I'd put in the work, mastered the drills, hit the weights, and stayed on the path. This is who I would be for the rest of my career: A disciple of Lenny Bias.

Lenny made a terrible decision and it cost him his life. My job was not just to survive the tragedy but to become better because of it. "The Man" gave me what I needed to succeed, everything from insights into which skills I had to improve to the pitfalls his death showed me I had to avoid. He's my shooting star, and I love him.

WALT

The season before my arrival in College Park, Coach Wade leads a courageous Terrapin team to an uplifting first-round NCAA Tournament victory over the University of California, Santa Barbara. A tightly contested second-round loss to the Kentucky Wildcats ends "The Dance" for Maryland, and as the final buzzer sounds, I slapped a new, crisp, saved-for-the-occasion red Terps hat on my head, tilted to the side, to memorialize my "members only" moment. A mixture of goose bumps and giddiness shook me as I considered my future.

The next time Maryland Basketball thrilled Cole Field House, I'd be on the court in a Terrapin uniform. Images of Len Bias explode in my imagination: in the black uniform, catching an alley-oop, shooting a jumper, smiling on draft night, and on the life-sized poster I'd only seen on television, the classic memento a Terrapin fan presented to Massenburg in 2014 at the final Maryland home game in the ACC.

I looked at the spot on the ceiling that I could not turn away from while I fought to process the loss of a legend and I can still feel tears retrace the tracks from 1986. Len Bias pointed the way to College Park and my fantastic future. That's a heavy debt on my heart, something I try to repay every day of my life. Swearing loyalty to the path "The Man" pointed out to me, I placed my Terp hat with precision next to a picture of Len and vowed to the young man in the mirror to turn grief into gold.

Losing Len Bias hurts, always, as much as if his crushing and heartbreaking death occurred only yesterday. To heal, the pain needed to burn into passion and transform me into a representative of the standard of excellence Len left in his legacy to the University of Maryland.

The life of Lenny Bias served as my blueprint for development. During the darkest times of reflection and introspection following his death, I faithfully studied the plan. A year in College Park as a full-time student and part-time athlete accelerates the healing of my emotional wounds and increases my need to express a dedication to a new life.

The question of who would sit in the Coach's office didn't matter.

In the fall of 1987, without delay and in the face of unprecedented adversity, Coach Wade recruited a group of highly competitive players to support the drive to bring Maryland back to where it belonged. Getting McDonald's All-Americans Steve Hood, Rodney Walker and Brian Williams, and Junior College All-American Rudy Archer to commit to Maryland told me Coach Wade wanted to win. I didn't question why he decided to hold me back from game action until after Christmas even though I was eligible in September. The newspapers said Coach wanted to see how my grades held up but they were wrong about so many things that I doubted the words. Maybe he wanted me to be hungrier, or angrier, or he needed the younger guys to gel, or he really thought it was best if I only practiced during the first semester. It added to the fire. I dominated the drills and scrimmages, did my homework, and waited. When my time came, I rejoined my Terps with a diminished sense of joy but highly motivated and determined to properly represent my Maryland.

I wanted to be the next Terp to bring "The House" down, another in a long line of great Maryland frontcourt players like Len Elmore, Tom McMillen, Charles "Buck" Williams, Ernest Graham, Albert King, Adrian Branch and, of course, Lenny Bias who carried Maryland to the top on their way to becoming NBA draft picks.

I returned to Cole Field House on December 28, 1987 to

play against the South Carolina Gamecocks. It had been three semesters since I'd been allowed to join the team on that sacred court and three semesters are a lifetime in the mind of a young college player.

The butterflies made it hard to go to sleep the night before the game. Four months passed by since my success in the Kenner League and even with my new, tougher physique and matching attitude, I couldn't help but worry. Twenty months had slipped away, and nothing prepares you for playing in a game except playing in a game. Time can be an enemy of confidence.

Even though Coach Wade had stocked the roster full of All-Americans, I was determined to break back into the starting lineup. I had to deal with learning new faces, new strengths, and new patterns but my day was coming.

I finally concentrated on Lenny, remembering some of his best games and running that replay of his incredible moves in my head. The butterflies disappeared and I got a couple of hours of sleep.

Running on a few bites of the pre-game meal, pent-up emotion, and pure adrenaline, I played the best game of my sophomore year. I felt like Lenny that night. Coach named me a starter and I dominated from the first minute. I scored four of the first eight points and rejected a shot to help put us up 20 to 11 early on. I took on the role of enforcer like I was born to. All the banging under the basket with the football players made the game easy and no one could stop me. In the second half, I owned both ends of the court. It was as close as I would ever come to Lenny's style of play and as I finished with twenty-five points and four blocked shots, you could have seen my smile from the top seats.

When the reporters asked me about the game, I praised my teammates: their iron will and sacrifice was what made this moment possible. In my heart, I dedicated this first game to Lenny Bias but I couldn't say that to the media. After the game, a year and a half after taking it down, I unrolled and re-hung my poster of Lenny. I only took it down again to hang it on a new wall.

In that year off, I changed for the better but I still wanted him there to see my improvement, my increased power, my new

confidence. I began to feel the extra bounce that comes from relentless weight work and I could see how it made Lenny both strong and quick. I worked on everything he used to do: jump hooks, two-dribble pull-ups, full court ball-handling drills, and jump shots from fifteen and eighteen feet out.

I took all the pain and suffering because of his passing and transformed it into an internal drive that still motivates me today. Because of Lenny, I gave Maryland everything: my best play, my best effort, my willingness to go the distance.

Everything.

Lenny Bias showed me the way.

I hopped into the fire during my first round of pickup games as a Terrapin matching up against our senior captain, Dave Dickerson, and after one day, I believed the Maryland coaches must be expert shooting instructors. Len Bias had the prettiest jumper of all, Adrian Branch could shoot, Dickerson has a sweet shot, Massenburg is automatic from the perimeter, each one is a frontcourt threat with a feathery touch. Weeks before my first college practice, before my first class as a Maryland student-athlete, my initiation into the Maryland Way through pickup ball gave me new confidence to complement the lessons. If I gave it my all, in time I'll be "nice" too and at least graduate from Maryland with a smooth jumper.

Being six-feet-eight inches tall and barely 165 pounds caused people to question my court position. People said I was too thin for the post and not quite right for conventional perimeter play. Comments like that couldn't have meant less to me; I played basketball to win, and my position was wherever I needed to be to make that happen. I was fortunate to have the constructive guidance and daily directives of Dickerson and fellow senior Greg Nared on how to manage life as a Maryland student-athlete, easing my transition from greenhorn to Diamondback. Dickerson and Nared were true examples of polished and determined success, real men who faced every situation with the maturity and focus of a professor.

Following Len to Maryland led me into a brave and extraordinary brotherhood. My veteran teammates, "Big Young'un," "Double D," and

"G-Nard," remained principled leaders and outstanding citizens who constantly reminded new players that there is life even after an incredible shooting star falls from the sky. Their perseverance formed a steady base for the rebirth of Maryland Basketball and offered me the privilege to enter College Park under a fraternal umbrella of protection.

We must.

We are Maryland.

Coach Wade introduced Walt to the team in the dining hall. I guess it was the new recruit's wiry frame that led Coach Wade to use the dinner table for a strength and conditioning conversation. Walt arrived with a reputation: a product of the P.G. County playgrounds, DC-certified, ready to take over the small forward position, score off the dribble, and shoot from three-point range with ease. Learning Walt chose Maryland because of Lenny Bias lets me know the freshman plays to honor a fallen idol, a feeling I know is capable of propelling talent to the top.

Jerrod Mustaf from famed DeMatha Catholic High School in Hyattsville, Maryland, only two miles from College Park, was the headliner of the 1988 freshman class, but the first time the team scrimmaged, the gangly guard/forward from Crossland High finished like a big man, with flair, making pinpoint passes look fundamental, leading his side to a lopsided win. Walt proved from the beginning that he could control a game, the crucial role of a true point guard. He put everyone in position, created offensive strategies at will, and only wanted to win. Walt flourished during the pre-season pickup games and his "I can play" attitude gave us a new look and new expectations.

I told Coach Wade right at the start that Walt should quarterback the team. We raised a few eyebrows and produced a potent inside-out recipe for a moment in Terrapin time. By the end of our first season in College Park together, avid Maryland fans shared my sentiment: Walt Williams was going to be someone special.

Maryland bringing in a distinguished, in-state national high school coach-of-the-year seemed more than suitable from my perspective. The image Coach Wade reflected on the Baltimore sidelines for the powerful Dunbar Poets reminded me of my father and grandfather: wise, stern, caring, and respected. Len Bias set my loyalty to College Park in solid bedrock and it felt as if having Coach Wade leading the program was a fantastic and unexpected bonus. Wade was known for helping disadvantaged kids, consistently winning, producing first-round NBA draft picks, and directing players toward successful careers outside the athletic arena which, to a wishful teenaged fan, more than satisfied my requirements for the job. Looking back, the tremendous triple challenge of replacing a legend the likes of Charles "Lefty" Driesell, picking up the pieces after Len's death, and absorbing the heat of being the first black head coach in the ACC was probably more than any single man or even an entire institution could meet.

During my season with Coach Wade, nearly three years after losing Len, we fought the bureaucracy of the ACC and the NCAA while stomaching and ignoring all the pundits who couldn't see us rising and the unrelenting chorus of jeers from what felt like a nation united against the Terrapin.

We endured. Coach Wade endured. The brazen disrespect strengthened my allegiance.

The experts portrayed us as a team in shambles and incapable of winning. Playing for a university and a region in doubt makes for tough times. We saw how the top sports publications ranked the Terps at the bottom and I felt they would have put us lower if possible. Just as success can lift a player and even an entire community to previously unknown heights, low expectations seemed to suck energy from our program, campus, and community.

We paid for it. We paid for playing at Maryland, being from Maryland, living in Maryland, and cheering for Maryland. We were down then, and that's why we're champions today.

Unaware of the significance when signing the letter of intent, putting on the Terrapin uniform we loved tagged us as scapegoats for all that was wrong, not just in the case of Len Bias but for every problem and scandal in college basketball and big-time sports. Unified by our unanimous drive to revive College Park, we banded under the Terrapin shell and pushed against the current to win for each other and the family of "Field House" faithful.

At the start of a pre-season practice, Coach Wade hears assistant coach Ralph Lee call me "Walt the Wizard" during a fast break drill. My teammate Jesse Martin took that Coach Lee remark and injected "Wizzie" Williams into the mix. The next time down the court I dished a no-look pass to Max Etienne for an easy lay-up, and Coach Wade shouted, "That's the Wizard." From that point forward Coach Wade called me "The Wizard" as often as he said my real name. At first, I thought Coach Wade said it because he was cool, tough, and able to relate. Minutes before our first scrimmage, my first as a Terrapin, Coach Wade told me he picked "The Wizard" because "Magic" already belonged to the Los Angeles Lakers.

I was blown away. For a skinny, streetball player to be linked to Earvin "Magic" Johnson was almost terrifying but, in the Maryland Way, I accepted the challenge to be "The Wizard" and return College Park to a place where champions play.

The rhythm created by kids on the playgrounds calling me "Walt, The Wizard" sounds normal for someone named Walter Williams, the way "Smooth" perfectly fits Sonny Smith and "Clyde, The Glide" rolls off the tongue. Coach Wade taps into the power of suggestion associated with alliterative nicknames by dubbing me "The Wizard" at eighteen, making everyone aware that he sees something unique. Coach Wade recognizing my skill set, real or imagined, and giving me the validation of a man I respected like family made me trust the confidence brewing inside. Maybe the code name evolved as part of a clever coaching ploy. By addressing me as "The Wizard," Coach Wade created an expectation and the image he projected parallels my attitude: crave greatness and make magic. I wanted to be Len Bias, an impossible dream, so Coach Wade turns the basketball into a wand and I thought of myself as "The Wizard," determined to reach the potential he saw in me.

"The Wizard" and I grew closer as teammates and friends, bonding during heartfelt discussions about our paths to the University of Maryland and the common denominator: our love for Lenny Bias. During our two years together as Terrapins, I developed the utmost respect for Walt, the man, and a friendship that has withstood the test of time. The loyalty Walt demonstrated by choosing to stay and play for the home team at a time when only questions marked its direction underlines his character.

Walt loves Maryland and just isn't the sort of person who abandons his friends and family when the going is tough. "The Wizard" remains the ultimate Marylander who best understands and appreciates the history and heritage of Terrapin Basketball. I believe the best teammate is one who loves the team more than himself. No one exhibited more love for the Terrapins than Walt Williams, the cornerstone, which is why "The Wizard" will always be deservedly embraced as a University of Maryland legend.

To say Walt joined us during a rebuilding process understates our dire circumstances. Jerrod Mustaf represented the future and I symbolized a polarizing link to the past. We needed a blue-chip backcourt ball artist who could play up to the caliber of Mustaf. Walt entered as a mystery and turned out to be the answer.

What position Walt should take on the court was always simple to me. He was the Playmaker. Put the ball in his hands. His signature socks pulled all the way up to the knees tell the rest of the story. Walt played basketball with style, standing out even in a star-studded Cole Field House as an instant trendsetter in fashion and performance. I recognized having a versatile, six-feet-eight perimeter player eliminating post double-teams as a terrific advantage over the competition, and a key to our success going forward. Jerrod Mustaf competes at the high level we expected. Walt develops into a jewel.

When practice officially kicked off, guys began to battle for precious playing time during the red versus white scrimmages and Walt exploded in front of our eyes, demonstrating a court awareness and a physical agility that only elevated the play of his teammates. Conversely, Walt was ultra-problematic for defenses.

True to his new nickname, Walt worked wizardry on the basketball court.

Power forwards and post players who are dependent upon perimeter spacing and teamwork identify and value a true playmaker that's always willing to "distribute the rock." Walt towered over most backcourt defenders and delivered the ball in rhythm, setting us up with silver-platter assists. If the opponent laid off him to help "the bigs" stop us, Walt could make shots from anywhere, discouraging his defender from double-teaming the post, and permitting one-on-one exploitations on the blocks for frontcourt players—an optimal "in the paint" scenario. Young Walt flashed reminders of a taller Keith Gatlin, always admired for his Terrapin pace, vision, and poise.

Maryland had a new star on the horizon.

Walt Williams landed in College Park on a valiant quest. To the delight of Maryland fans everywhere, Walt turned into "The Wizard," and changed the way the world looked at Maryland Basketball, all in honor of "The Man from Landover."

Excited with the combination of ACC rookie sensation Brian Williams, Massenburg, my classmate Jerrod Mustaf, and a solid backcourt, I thought the future of Maryland Basketball looked bright in 1988. Instead, we struggled. I persevered through the disappointment, matured as a player and as a man, earned the team's respect, and worked into the starting lineup to get the best of the invaluable Division One schooling.

Just when it felt like we were committed to bouncing back, Coach Wade resigned.

No one fully understands the loss of a beloved teammate as did Massenburg and the senior members of the 1988-1989 Terrapins. They were eighteen and living in the nightmare. My grief paled when measured against their feelings and I loved Len Bias more than most. Shaped in the firestorm that swept over College Park after Len's death, they were ideal mentors for the next generation of Terps, more than strong enough to pull us through another disturbance. The lessons they taught during every conversation pointed us to good judgment, true brotherhood, and being a light in the calm when all is said and done.

Terrapin lesson number one: victory in basketball is a byproduct of great decisions. Swap "basketball" for "life" and you have an excellent formula for success.

Never-ending media focus on a team wearily concluding a season with nine wins and twenty losses raises suspicions and rumblings of things gone wrong. Amid the whispers and rumors, I decided Coach Wade never had a chance. Hired during one of the worst periods in the history of Maryland sports as the University was reeling from Len's death, I think his chances for long-term success were slim from the start. I wish I could have done more but all I could do was play better.

News trucks filled the lot behind Cole Field House and strangers in suits stalked the campus with microphones and recorders in hand. The commotion fed on itself. That many reporters must mean there's a story somewhere. It's the same theory you usually hear about politics: where there's smoke, there's fire. The only story from us would have been a piece on survival.

As new and shocking headlines seemed to appear almost daily, I fell back into a paralyzing emotional detachment that contaminated my perspective on the present and the future.

In the end, Bob Wade was my coach, the coach of my Maryland Terrapins, a man who believed in me, and suddenly he was gone. My coach, my mentor, and our leader: gone. Maryland relapsed into a state of anxiety as we all worried about the future and wondered what calamity would smack us next.

Family means the world to me. My Maryland team became "family" the moment I signed the letter of intent to attend the University. The hard times we encountered during my freshman year united us and at the end of the season we pledged to turn things around. Admiring his sincerity and his expressed objective to raise the Terrapin flag, I expected Coach Wade to lead the charge.

Bob Wade, educator, trailblazer, Baltimore legend, and National Football League veteran sat for hours in my living room assuring my parents that Maryland would prove to be the best for me both academically and athletically. Coach Wade stressed discipline in the classroom as a requirement for young men to become good student-athletes and great citizens, describing basketball as a vehicle for us to develop into exemplary men. My parents trusted this man that the University of Maryland selected to head the basketball program and believed in his good intentions. We bonded because his concern for our family stretched beyond basketball. Coach Wade demonstrated a strong belief in every player's value outside of athletics and preached that winning could only be achieved by preparing to succeed in life once the ball stops bouncing. He was a man I regarded as far more than just another basketball coach.

The resignation of Coach Wade struck a sour note with me. The disconcerting process added insult to a complicated injury and extended my aggravation all the way to animosity. My coach was family. He'd given me the precious opportunity to live my dream of playing for my University. As a teenager, I suffered through sleepless nights to play basketball for the University of Maryland. Because Coach Bob Wade said so, I am a Terrapin, gracious and unwilling to pretend anyone coaching the Maryland basketball team in 1988 would have offered me a scholarship.

Bob Wade was a stable point in our unstable universe.

Now he's gone.

A clear explanation for the Coach Wade resignation might have altered my opinion. To resign after only three seasons, I figured his departure must have resulted from yet more fallout from Len's death. With findings and reports and inquests swirling around campus, the task of returning the Maryland basketball program to glory seemed like an overwhelming challenge for whoever followed in the shadow of Coach "Lefty" Driesell.

One of the last newspaper articles I remember reading after Coach Wade resigned was written by Tony Kornheiser of the Washington Post.

In the piece, he called Bob Wade the wrong choice from the beginning and said we were right back to where we were in 1986: ground zero. After a deep breath to clear out the scathing sentiment, I watched the dust settle, and crafted a plan to improve my view of the world. I stopped reading opinion columns about Maryland and paid little attention to the media even when the coverage turned positive. I know the chaos and pain of 1989 was incomparable to losing Len Bias and enduring the devastating summer of 1986. Today, when I hear Mr. Kornheiser speak on television or the radio, it reminds me how far off-base I considered his 1989 position, even though, as an outside observer, he might have been correct.

Starting over with another head coach turns out to be the least troublesome aspect of the transition. Floundering without direction for a month nearly destabilizes a solid season of teambuilding and reclamation groundwork. Massenburg was the personification of a senior team leader, providing a steadying presence, setting up workout schedules to center our focus on improving instead of fretting about things we had no control over.

The only answers regarding the future of Maryland Basketball popped up in print or on television. On June 13, 1989, we learned from news reports that the head coach from Ohio State University, a former Terrapin player, would replace Coach Bob Wade at the University of Maryland. His résumé highlighted our new leader as having recruited All-American Jimmy Jackson to Ohio State and having succeeded in the tough Big East with Boston College and locally at American University.

More than anything, I respected his shameless loyalty to Maryland Basketball.

Time allowed my anger to subside and I recognized the need to separate emotions that surfaced because of the Coach Wade crisis from my personal need to make the best decision for my future. I focused on three points: the type of coach coming in, whether the new coach wants me to stay at Maryland, and how his system affects the probability of maximizing my potential. I completed the mandatory homework, learned of the possibility to transfer without sacrificing eligibility, and researched other programs where my talents might flourish. The Coach Wade resignation aggravated my Terrapin shell and the irritation drove me to consider walking away from my true love for this betrayal and for the manner in which they discarded a man I admired.

With my belief in Maryland more vulnerable than ever, I could only foresee another painful period in limbo, a new coach, and never-ending media abuse. I never expected the new setback that was to come.

Chapter 7

MOVING UP WITH **GARY WILLIAMS**

In the spring of 1989, Gary Williams returns to lead his alma mater.

Tony Massenburg becomes the only Terrapin to play for Driesell, Wade, and Williams.

Walt Williams comes to Maryland in 1988 and stays.

WALT

I remember Coach Williams on the Boston College sidelines during the Big East Games of the Week going toe-to-toe with larger-than-life coaches like future Hall of Famers Lou Carnesecca of St. John's, Jim Boeheim of Syracuse, and Georgetown's John Thompson, Jr. Finding out Gary Williams led Maryland as point guard and captain "back in the day" was the clincher. Coach Williams was coming home and I saw him as the type of man who believed that regardless of the consequences, the moment in time, or the stage of his life, when the people at home need your help, you don't ask questions, you come home.

Coach Williams arrived sporting his Terrapin shell with confidence and we recognized his passion as genuine. He told us we would win a national championship at Maryland and I believed him. He outlined a vision of Maryland Basketball returned to its rightful place among the elite, and demonstrated the courage necessary to get there with an aggressive delivery that mirrored the electric obsession burning beneath my Terrapin jersey. He told us of his own agony, the pain he felt as he watched his Terps suffer after the nightmare of Len's death and the inquisition that followed.

Coach Williams may have been motivated to leave a good job in Columbus, Ohio by many factors. I chose to believe he wanted to return to College Park because no school shines brighter than the alma mater. Like me, he loves Maryland, and Terps go all the way for what we love.

The University of Maryland appointed Coach Gary Williams as the "new sheriff in town." I applied to become the deputy.

Coach Williams assembled a skilled staff, defined each player's role in the recovery, and we went to work. Every member of our program—administrators, managers, walk-ons, and the scholarship student-athletes—took charge of a piece of the puzzle and demonstrated an iron-clad determination to elevate Terrapin Basketball. Players applied newly acquired leadership skills on the court, in the classroom, and in the community. We grew into a solid family, entering each game sure of our mission, and certain we were on the right path. We represented Maryland and Maryland responded by showing up to let us know they had our backs.

Our first three conference games under Coach Williams took place in Cole Field House: we beat Wake Forest in game one and a week later stunned North Carolina and presented our new coach his first ACC victory against the celebrated Dean Smith. It was an early warning to all elite teams to "Fear the Turtle" and resulted in a whispering campaign that the Terps were going to be thoroughly competitive. Two tough losses during the 1989-1990 season to Duke, including an overtime thriller with the fourth-ranked Blue Devils, solidified our resolution.

We were moving up. We will win. Maryland Basketball has survived unbelievable misfortune and is now turning past two pages of adversity to begin a chapter we can write with a new perspective. Then the hammer fell.

Shortly after a two-point second-round loss in the National Invitation Tournament ends the 1989-1990 season—our first season under Coach Williams—the NCAA hands down harsh penalties against Maryland Basketball for violations perpetrated by the previous administration.

The bottom line: No coverage of Maryland games on live television and no post-season tournament play.

Ouch!

Whatever the rationale for these ruthless punishments, the ripples of despair that moved through the Maryland community had a disturbing feeling of déjà vu. First Len Bias dies, then Coach Driesell resigns, followed by Coach Wade, and now we get hit by painful sanctions.

Will Coach Williams resign and complete the cycle of disaster?

Two harsh blows against the Maryland spirit in my first two seasons in College Park make me think anything could happen next.

The next thing was an absolute barrage of telephone calls from rival coaches and universities informing me that I was destined to be the missing piece that would solve their championship puzzle. All of them, subtly or blatantly, highlighted the latest sanctions, pointed out how they could negatively affect my future, and mentioned the convenient clause that would allow me to transfer to another school without having to sit out a year. Guys I knew in the NBA said I should just say goodbye to college life and head for "The League."

Wow!

Years later, on February 7, 2006, Coach Gary Williams made history with a total of 349 Terrapin victories, passing the innovator, Coach Charles "Lefty" Driesell, and ensuring himself a permanent seat at the top of Maryland Basketball.

In his post-game comments, Coach Williams spoke about how important it was that a young man named Walt Williams chose to stay with the Terrapin Basketball program even after the sanctions knocked us flat. I was humbled and honored by his words but the fact is I only played a small role in rebuilding the Terrapin community. Through all those tough, exhausting years of constant mayhem and slashing criticism, Maryland fans, students, players, and coaches showed their unyielding courage and loyalty, holding on to the belief that we would win, that our school, our state, and our teams would come out of the storm the champions we knew in our hearts we were.

In other words, we would emerge…Terrapins.

I stayed with Maryland because I believe loyalty is a supreme virtue and "being true" is always the best choice. I needed to be true and satisfy the sixteen-year-old kid inside, the boy who wanted to be like Len Bias, and walk the path that would make College Park, Maryland the special place I always felt it was.

No one with roots in the Washington, DC region will ever forget losing Len or the narrative painted by his too-short twenty-two years of life.

He moves us and so we carry on.

We absorbed the sanctions, put the carnage in the rearview mirror, and never stopped fighting, improving, and learning. Slowly, painfully, we recovered the reputation we'd earned under the leadership of Coach Driesell. In the course of this quarter-century mission, the University of Maryland rose from the shadows of gloom and doubt into a world-class institution with a championship basketball program. If taken as just another challenge to meet with courage and determination, even the worst adversity leads to increased personal strength and athletic proficiency. Accepting the very real and very painful lessons of our past strengthened the Terrapin shell and pointed the way forward. We are Maryland and we only triumph when we succeed together.

Loyalty prevails.

TONY

Graduation was the only thing I expected of my senior year at Maryland. Another coach was gone, the media onslaught continued, and I needed to fight every day to make it to "The League." Three coaches in five years made for internal and external turmoil exacerbated by the manner in which Bob Wade was shown the door. That revolving door made it harder to follow the path but I kept pushing.

I just wanted the new coach to see me in action, to feel my desire to be the best player in the ACC, and to know my teammates and I wore Maryland across our chests with pride.

The exceptional potential of sophomores Walt "The Wizard" and Jerrod Mustaf gives me the nerve to believe we could win. Gutsy Gary Williams, the "coach who can," walks into Cole Field House and agrees. He stepped up, leaned on the leaders in the locker room, and molded a philosophy around what works on the court. Coach Williams brought back the grit that "Lefty" and

Lenny built into Maryland Basketball. We talked about playing tough, forging a continuous movement upward, and never forgetting our duty to re-establish Maryland's elite status. Coach Williams recognized the load each teammate of Lenny Bias carried; he felt it in a deeply personal way, and he let me know that he, too, was wounded by the merciless negative publicity smearing Maryland and its basketball team. Integrity needed to be built into the foundation of present-day Maryland.

We would recover. We would be back better than ever.

Gary Williams left a winning program at Ohio State to come *home* and lead his Maryland family into a war on the courts to prove ourselves against a sports world that had turned against us. He knew we must embrace being in the trenches in order to rise. He had only one requirement: demonstrate every day your commitment to restoring Maryland Basketball to its rightful position.

We demonstrated our appreciation for this united front by executing the plan and, nine months later, earned a spot in the 1990 post-season, an anxiety-relieving message to our fans that the new and improved Maryland Terrapins could and would win.

To a deeply grief-stricken Terrapin Nation, these first steps on the journey beyond misery appeared to be insurmountable. Coach Williams invested every bit of his soul in us and the team could feel an enthusiasm for Maryland Basketball equaling, possibly surpassing, his passion for coaching, an alluring characteristic making us want to play for him.

Stay Maryland. Stay tough. Come out winners.

It's the course fixed by Lenny Bias.

Coach Williams pushed us into an ultra-aggressive up-tempo brand of basketball. Being the underdog backed into a corner gave us the strength and the passion to go shot-for-shot with every team in the powerhouse ACC. We made them fight for every inch they moved up the court—everywhere, every time.

We earned a new reputation: the Terps will pressure you until we wear you down and then pressure you some more. Duke and North Carolina would occasionally extend their defense beyond the three-point arc for a limited time. Other teams within the top-ranked conference employed pressure defenses to try to change momentum.

We started games in full-court press mode and fought to cause havoc until the final buzzer, playing the sort of tough all-over defense that resulted in turnover opportunities. This wide-open style suited our intense desire to win for the Terrapin Nation and allowed us to force the issue on defense, isolate mismatches to generate offense, and play to our strengths.

It wasn't basketball strategy as much as heartfelt determination in action.

Some analysts, focusing on the physical nature of basketball, said we weren't as talented as the other teams. Far more important than the view from the press box was the respect we gained from our peers, the men we played against. They learned that we were never going to give up and we would battle for every moment of every game. With that respect, we built a firm competitive foundation for future Terrapins to inherit.

If you're playing Maryland, expect to dance for the full forty minutes.

Although the season was clouded by impending penalties from the three-year Wade regime, Coach Williams gave us a clear sense of purpose and we responded with everything we had. Anchored by senior captain Tony "Massive," as I affectionately call Massenburg, our play generates a positive momentum, eighteen energizing wins, and a strong close down the stretch deserving of a first-class invitation to the NCAA Championship Tournament. Seventeen wins had been enough for the 1988 Terrapins to enter the NCAA Tournament. Eighteen ought to meet 1990 requirements.

Moments after the end of the ACC Tournament, the initial, unofficial sanction lands: Maryland is relegated to the Junior Varsity and will play in the National Invitation Tournament (NIT) with a hint that we are unwelcome in "March Madness."

Deflation.

Possessed by our past and a bond with Coach Williams, we revived our fan base with twelve home victories, finishing the 1989-1990 regular season winning five of our final six games, historically a record that would guarantee acceptance into the varsity post-season competition.

A guarantee for most, but not for Maryland.

Once again, I sit across from Massenburg and wonder how often he reassesses his decision to stick with Maryland. Tony dominated his senior year, stacking up prime-time statistics with double-digit points and rebounds for the entire season, excelling in the rarefied Terrapin air. We were a Cinderella squad, a formidable unit that the majority of the nation couldn't or wouldn't recognize.

But Cinderella could dream and here's mine: our "Big Four" at the West Regional tangling up teams who have no idea what we can do. At six-feet-ten inches tall, Cedric Lewis blocks shots and controls the lane. A commanding six-feet-nine, two-hundred and forty pounds, Tony "Massive" dominates power forwards. Jerrod Mustaf at six-feet-ten inches tall can play small forward, displaying his superior perimeter skills, and I'm a six-feet-eight point guard with Teyon McCoy pumping in uncontested three-point baskets from around the arc. Imagine the 1990 Terrapins on CBS television with Brent Musburger and Billy Packer speaking positively about the resurgent Maryland program, and the powerful influence the national exposure would have brought to rebuilding.

Imagine them if you can because you can't relive games that never happened.

Sanctions: our fate required we take them like men. The first sanctions hit hard and the real penalties were still to come. It felt so wrong but we sucked it up and did our jobs.

The ruling prohibiting us from participating in any post-season play and banning us from live television landed with an impact capable of destroying a weaker team's will to compete. Outsiders could be excused if they asked us, "Why bother to play at all?"

Being slapped with such a severe penalty felt malicious when we considered the alleged infractions. In our locker room, an emotional consensus emerged. We were four years beyond the nightmare and the dissection of Maryland Basketball under the microscope of atonement continued.

The NCAA actions seemed biased.

The punitive practice of hamstringing a new coach for the failures of a previous administration can have irreversible effects. Being ineligible to play in the National Tournament and compete for a championship challenged our mettle, but we trusted if we stood proud and played strong, people would realize, "Maryland belongs."

Television did not matter to me. The size of the arena and the stage setting rarely served as a motivating factor. I played the game to claim victory, and if the NCAA slotted our games at six in the morning on an island west of Alaska, I would approach each contest with the same must-win mindset. Once more, we formed a wall with our shells under the Maryland flag and focused on the precious opportunities to compete within the ACC, at that time acknowledged to be the best conference in America. Thundering along Tobacco Road registers on the national level and people begin to notice, tape-delayed or printed in the next day's paper. Facing sanctions, college basketball reverts to its purest form: Play to win.

I could do that.

A failure to mesh early in our first season under Coach Williams results in a demoralizing loss to Coppin State College, but the setback proves instrumental in our development as a team and my personal evolution as a playmaker. Coppin State succeeded in pressuring and trapping our guards, shutting down passing lanes, and effectively stalling our offense. The dual edges of an in-state loss and a true "gut-check" practice on the following day triggers a drastic request on my part.

I went to Coach Williams and, highlighting my time playing point guard as a freshman Terp, painted a novel path to victory: move me from the front court and allow me to take over the primary ball-handler position to create the angles that meant easier shots for Massenburg and Jerrod Mustaf. Coach Williams gave me a silent nod, patted me on the back, and I walked into the locker room wondering if he thinks I'm a know-it-all.

Even more, I wondered if he sees the game the way I see it.

Coach whistled the start of practice number two after the Coppin State debacle and announced, "We're scrimmaging, first team on offense."

I shuffled toward the baseline with Massenburg to man the small forward position, excited to go right into five on five instead of another day of exhausting drills. Coach Williams tossed the ball to me and with that, gives me the keys to the play-making position, and tells the scout squad to apply maximum pressure. I dominated the floor.

Coach Williams sampled my reaction to stress and I won his trust, the point guard spot, and the chance to evolve as "The Wizard." We caught fire and won the next five games on course to a triumphant season. We deserved an invitation to the NCAA Tournament. An ACC team winning eighteen games including impressive victories over tournament-bound teams says we can play. We are worthy of being bracketed in the "Big Dance." One thing was clear: The new decade will see a Terrapin rising.

Walking across the stage as a graduate from the University of Maryland marks the end of an era: The last teammate of "The Man" beats the odds. More than anything, it was an intensely personal victory that tested me to the breaking point and taught me how to dig for determination and find persistence. Making the honor roll and graduating feels as great as any triumph on the basketball court.

All veteran basketball players learn that there is only so long you can continue to play, a wonderful opportunity for sure, but for every year that passes after the dance is over and the trophies tarnish, an education becomes more essential for survival. As the last of Len's teammates to play at Maryland, sometimes I felt like I majored in Survival with all the attacks, smear campaigns, and sanctions. Perhaps we all did because being tough enough to survive anything was just one of the legacies we inherited from "The Man."

Memories of my time with Lenny flooded my mind throughout my final season as a Terrapin. I stopped merely *thinking* of Lenny Bias. I *channeled* him by practicing and playing with the same relentless determination I'd seen Lenny practice and perform, and by attempting to emulate his determination to dominate. Off the court, I survived because the lesson teaches accountability, and I tried to repay Maryland, my teammates, and Coach Williams with my humble rendition of "The Man from Landover."

Before my final game, Coach Williams comforted my parents

with kind words of appreciation for my ability to lead and my success as a role model, praising my service as a positive example for the younger players on the team and Maryland's way going forward. As I looked at Walt, smiling and clapping, happy for me and with the direction of the program, glad to be a Terp, I thought of being a freshman looking at Lenny. He's there at every turn. His example affects everything.

The Jerrod Mustaf declaration to leave Maryland for the NBA after our sophomore year deals a huge blow to the team, another jab we need to absorb. Replacing our leader Massenburg and his Herculean performances would be a daunting task even with Mustaf but the dual departure strips the cupboard bare. On the other hand, a call from the NBA is sweet music in the ears of any college basketball player—just check the number of underclassmen declaring for the draft every year.

Watching on television the formal elevation of Jerrod Mustaf and Tony Massenburg from the University of Maryland into "The League" during the 1990 NBA draft raised the team's spirits out of our sanction-based depression. All of us cheered as our teammates, more importantly our brothers, received top-fifty acceptance as official members of "The League."

Seeing Massenburg in the warm-up line with the San Antonio Spurs, wearing the NBA uniform made popular by the smooth styling of my childhood favorite, George "The Iceman" Gervin, causes a tingling today just the way it wowed me in October 1990. Massenburg epitomized sheer persistence as he hammered through disorder and forged his path to being a great college player, an honor roll graduate from the University of Maryland, and a world-class athlete.

Up until the 1990 NBA draft, I focused solely on destroying the competitor in front of me in the streets, on the playgrounds, and within the ACC. Becoming an NBA player was a distant wish, remotely possible only if I could achieve two attainable but difficult goals: be the best I could be and make Maryland a champion. Watching my teammates, my boys, wearing NBA jerseys inspired me to consider a future in the pros. Because of the ticket to the NBA earned by Mustaf and Massenburg, my perception of my potential expanded, leading to a priceless experience, a revelation, and a limitless tomorrow.

Without Massenburg and Mustaf, we expected tough going but the haymaker sanctions levied by the NCAA hit us like a mule kick to the back of the head. Abandoning Maryland was never an option, so we settled in for combat against uncharted adversity.

Coach Williams approached competing without Massenburg and Mustaf through the articulation of a memorandum: regardless of the opposition, even if the scholarships originate from the Triangle region of North Carolina, we are Maryland, and we have Walt Williams, so bring it.

In the midst of a poor shooting night during the early portion of the 1990-1991 season, I decide against taking an open shot, and instead, pass the ball laterally to set up a teammate. Seconds later, Coach Williams, irate, calls a time out. As I turn for the bench, he meets me on the court and says, "If you don't shoot, we can't win." That stunning green light for scoring changes the tone of the game, and the future of Maryland Basketball.

Electrified and inspired, leaping from the huddle liberated, I rose to a new level. The head Terrapin expressing confidence in my ability to "get buckets" frees the streetwise ball player in me, that self-confident scrappy kid who won that all-important scholarship. Coach Williams trusted us to execute our roles as soldiers in the struggle to advance Maryland, one possession at a time. I needed to lead, exceed, and strive to be the best at all times. Having the chief openly believe in me strengthens the unit. His endorsement of my competence to pilot our team provides the license to take control and the power to act like "The Wizard."

The passion Coach Williams feels for Maryland and his will to revive the basketball program spreads among us like a second chance in a longstanding love affair. Coach Williams motivates from the heart with a point guard mentality for positioning players to succeed, highly effective traits proven to maximize Terrapin potential, and key factors that allowed me to thrive.

Crafty coaching and selfless teammates place me in a position to represent the United States of America during the 1991 Pan American Games in Havana, Cuba. With national media outlets assembling at Cole

Field House for interviews regarding my good fortune, I planned for the predictable questions and tough comments about Len Bias. I wanted someone to ask about Len and give me a moment to sing his praises and tell the masses why Len Bias will remain a driving force in my life.

No one even mentions Len, evidence of another page turning.

The Pan Am Games invitation was an individual honor I accepted with apprehension, still leery of the spotlight. Fear of the selection committee looking at "From Maryland" in my biography and seeing only "College Park 1986" in their minds tempered the excitement of making the final cut to wear a USA jersey. I worried that five years might not be enough time for America to accept without reservations a University of Maryland basketball player donning the red, white, and blue.

The crippling sanctions distorted my sense of fairness but the Pan Am invitation set up the perfect occasion to show the country how Maryland rebounds from adversity. I arrived at the Team USA Basketball training center in Colorado Springs, Colorado sporting Terrapin gear from head to toe.

Here I am.

Maryland. Love us now or later, we're here.

Moments after College Basketball Hall of Fame Coach Gene Keady congratulates me for winning a spot on Team USA, a reporter asks for my thoughts on going from a relative unknown to a possible starter in the world theater. The verbal response comes from a split-second celebration of being an unknown, just an American basketball player, and includes an appropriate sample of the emotions rolling within: humility, respect, exhilaration.

To express the infinite significance of a Crossland High School Terp carrying the American flag in Cuba and my role as a messenger for a bounce-back University of Maryland, I gave a first-class performance in pursuit of a gold medal. By choosing a Terrapin to wear "The Colors" of our country, the Team USA selection committee, Coach Keady, and his staff make a global statement announcing the return of the Terrapin, and I feel the gray clouds above my community start to thin. USA Basketball deems the University of Maryland legitimate and people notice a P.G. County Terp winning on the court and in the classroom. I imagine building on the momentum and leading the way for the second chance that Maryland deserves.

The Pan Am Games opened my eyes to a new kind of inspiration: patriotism. Being considered one of the twelve best college players in the country, practicing with the nation's top talent, and competing against seasoned veterans of international acclaim proves Terrapin tenacity succeeds at the highest level. Experts and chatterboxes amplified the noise about my readiness for the NBA but the possibility of a special senior season and the fantasy of a packed Cole Field House welcoming the Tar Heels and National Champion Blue Devils to College Park for old-fashioned ACC showdowns outshine the need to leave early for "The League."

Teaming in the ultimate all-for-one occasion in Cuba with Christian Laettner, Thomas and Grant Hill of Duke, and Eric Montross of North Carolina boasting "USA" on our jerseys produces mutual respect between natural enemies. The Terrapins reclaimed a familiar distinction: Home of World-Class Ball Players. Going forward, from Tobacco Road and beyond, an intensifying fear of turtles grips college basketball.

Our case is one of classic desensitization: Marylanders and Terrapins suffered through terrible misfortune but every ounce of adversity and vilification thrown at us only increased our resistence to disruption. Bitter memories of the Bias heartbreak, the Driesell displacement, the transfer of prized-talent Brian Williams, the resignation of Coach Wade, and the ramifications from the loss of live television and post-season tournaments blistered my shell. During the grueling process to keep the flagship afloat, our best returning big man Jerrod Mustaf decides to forgo his college eligibility and enter the NBA.

Normal did not exist, only conditioned expectations.

No Massenburg, no Mustaf, no one watching, and no chance for "March Madness."

Friends, teammates, coaches, family, and every local media outlet freely expressed their opinions about my choices: stay at Maryland through the fire; listen to the NBA insiders and head for "The League"; transfer to the University of Anywhere Else and play on the national scene with a shot at a title.

Along with coaches courting and calling from all parts of the country, people spewed about the cloud parked over Maryland, and the limited television exposure hindering my development. To escape the hurricane and refocus on my path, I went home to Temple Hills.

To my surprise, but totally in character, Coach Williams followed and his simple statement, "The ball is in your hands," echoes loudly.

Coach Williams and Coach Billy Hahn, also a Terrapin and a member of the great Maryland teams of the early '70s, came to our house with a plan for my parents to consider. I listened, thinking of the ball in my hands leading the Cole Field House crew to victory. Other schools kept knocking. Georgetown has a natural and proximal attraction. Joining the Virginia Cavaliers would allow me to stay close to home and remain in the ultra-competitive ACC. Hall of Fame Coach Jerry Tarkanian and the NBA-ready Running Rebels in Las Vegas looked like a slam dunk. Each time my logical mind convinces me to head for another school, my heart speaks out against it, and in the end, it all came down to me hurting for Maryland and wanting to play a part in ending the pain.

Len Bias turned me into a Terp and to take off the shell to play for another university would mean giving up on the beliefs that lifted me into the opportunity. Only halfway through our first season together, Coach Williams gambled and let a rangy forward play point guard and be the playmaker for his team. He believed in Maryland and he believed in me. The role he created for me to be "The Wizard" clears my path to follow "The Man."

We stayed together because we love Maryland. Loyalty rewards.

Summer, 1989: A young ball player introduces himself as Johnny Rhodes from Dunbar High School in DC and says he wants to talk Terps. Neighborhood and blacktop chatter pegs Johnny a potential all-time great. A second conversation while shooting hoops with the conscientious lefty changes Maryland Basketball.

Johnny loved Len Bias, named me his favorite player, and considered accepting a scholarship to join me in College Park. The importance of having a star from "The District" playing for Maryland pops into my mind right away. Some who grew to love the Terps because of local stars like Adrian Branch and "The Man from Landover" turned their backs on the Terrapins during the thorny phase. Johnny Rhodes committing to and flourishing in College Park would encourage the urban coalition to remember Maryland.

McDonald's All-American Duane Simpkins and high-flying Exree Hipp joined Rhodes as prime local targets, the "DMV Three," and when they visited campus during recruitment, I communicated two points of interest. First, Coach Williams uses agitation to stimulate effort and pushes all your buttons to insure we execute the X's and O's, so don't mistake his sideline antics for madness. After a harmonic sigh of relief, the trio confessed high admiration for the unbridled passion Coach exhibits, the genuineness of his devotion to making Maryland Basketball great, and the freedom for players to express individual talent in the up-tempo, Terrapin-in-your-face style of play that Coach Williams endorses.

The second message I gave to the recruits yielded the greatest impact. I focused on getting the "Big Three" to appreciate the historical significance of their role in revitalizing our area and healing the battered hearts of Maryland fans everywhere. We walked through campus exploring their unique opportunity: they could play at home, provide the triple combination the University needed to knock down the last door, and continue the re-creation of a program that the region would love and the country would respect.

We talked about Len Bias. They wanted to learn all I remembered about "The Man," and I wanted them to understand his effect on the "DMV" and the game we love. Len going from Landover to the top of college basketball builds up the confidence of every playground kid on the streets of Washington, DC and its suburbs and leads them to believe they can make it as well. I shared with the prospective Terps the sweetness of succeeding in front of friends and relatives, and the advantages of the strong support system at Maryland, strumming the native chord. I reminded them of our kinship and the privileged option to enact their inalienable right as heirs of the family business, to grow it forward, and I could see each of them thinking of home as they nodded "yes."

They knew.

They felt the void created by the loss of Len Bias. They recognized the effect their unity and commitment to College Park would have on their community, and so the "DMV Three" stepped up and took a stand to cement critical positions in the Maryland resurrection.

Halloween, 1992: A local trio suits up for the University of Maryland to treat Naismith Hall of Fame Ambassador Dick Vitale and ten-thousand revelers to a rousing "Midnight Madness," and sets the foundation of Terrapin Basketball deep into the bedrock of Maryland's soul.

History will show that the 1989-1992 teams helped Coach Williams and Maryland build a bridge over a tumultuous tide. Johnny Rhodes, Duane Simpkins, and Exree Hipp are the first three bricks connecting that bridge to the road leading my Maryland toward the program-defining national championship.

Before finishing my playing career at Maryland, the staff identified two more bricks to link with the "DMV Three" for a rock-solid unit. The coaches described these two as "must-gets," the post presence necessary to win it all, a bruiser All-American from Baltimore and a sleeper from nearby Norfolk, Virginia. I considered the kid from "B-more" a Terp from the start. Being from Maryland, I thought getting Keith Booth to commit would be an easy sell. Snatching the Norfolk youngster from the Virginia Cavaliers or the Virginia Tech Hokies could be a challenge.

Blind loyalty caused me to forget the resentment Baltimore had for the Terrapins because of Bob Wade's treatment in College Park. I assumed Keith Booth yearned for College Park the way, in my mind, all Maryland "hoopsters" did. It still feels wrong whenever a basketball player from Maryland goes to another school after being offered a scholarship to play for the University of Maryland. The wall between Baltimore and College Park was long-standing but Coach Williams broke through it, attended some of the Dunbar Poets' games during their incredible winning streak, and Keith Booth followed him back to Maryland and healed the rift.

What I discovered about Joe Smith, the Virginia recruit, wows me still. Smith considered me the player he most admired and even sported my signature knee-high socks in tribute. Amazing! I made an impact on the life of a young man in the way Len Bias influenced me. The awesome revelation made me determined to put a Terrapin red jersey on that Virginia kid even if I had to play one-on-one against Ralph Sampson and Dell Curry to win him over.

Mr. Smith goes to Maryland.

The make-up of our 1989-1992 teams fit the times: scrappy, more blacktop than black tie, with an uncompromising demand for respect. We couldn't predict or modify the severity of the sanctions, so we pledged to restore the Terrapin brand by going all out against Duke and North

Carolina, champion blue-bloods, trusting that real basketball fans will admire our trademark determination even without the bright lights and confetti. National exposure never factored into our equation for success. Standing strong against the ACC and the circumstances provided the winning platform for College Park to recover, be competitive, and build. The new Maryland Basketball started with a group of good guys who knew how to fight, exactly what the University needed. We sacrificed to be Terrapins. We played to prove we can.

Maryland moved closer to turning another page with each pre-season accolade before my senior year. Naturally, Duke played a major role in the 1991-1992 season, adding contour to the promising resurrection of our program. The Blue Devils entered Cole Field House as the number one team in the country, and we relished the chance to chop down the undisputed kings of college basketball.

In a brilliant scheme of anticipation, Coach Williams moved me to shooting guard and opted for Kevin McLinton to be our lead ball handler and plate-setter to beat the early traps Coach knew Duke would employ. The switch redefined us, allowing me to attack aggressively on the offensive end and requiring my amazing teammates to adopt a new mission: free "The Wizard."

McLinton develops into a marvelous floor-general; the team meshes within the new offense, and Maryland gets a red-letter ride on the shoulders of a fearless generation of Terrapins. Coach Williams added wrinkles to the playbook to accentuate our talents and challenged our resolve to meet our potential. We were the Maryland student-athletes charged with moving beyond a cruel moment. The University needed us to complete our appointed duty for it to move on so, in true Terrapin fashion, our determination led us to compete at our highest level regardless of perception, penalties, and sanctions.

> *"Walt Williams scoring thirty points in seven straight conference games meant we could compete, we could win. It gave us the national attention we needed to keep moving forward and it led to 11 consecutive tournament appearances."*
>
> *—Hall of Fame Coach Gary Williams*

Walking around College Park during the record-setting seven-game streak through the ACC, surrounded by an upbeat Terrapin family in unison, witnessing the campus-wide release of a deeply suppressed vibrancy, the goal seems within reach.

We have the right to cheer again.

At the end of my Maryland career, I wanted people to say, "Len Bias and Walt Williams." Because coaches Williams, Hahn, Art Perry, and Jimmy Patsos structured the offense in my favor and my teammates were willing to trust and follow the game plan, people listened to the new noise from College Park, and a fortunate kid from Crossland could be "The Wizard."

During our streak of games where a player scored thirty or more points, the exceptional performances by my teammates often went unnoticed. The teams and coaches we competed against counted on me taking most of our shots and probably watched film of us in action to counter our options. Having teammates execute our strategy to perfection made the difference. Without fearless team defense, selfless screen-setting, and hard cuts to the basket freeing me for clean looks at the rim, the streak would never have happened.

Whenever someone mentions our record-setting run, I point to the essential role of the team when one player stands out. We needed the superpowers of Kevin McLinton and Vince Broadnax to checkmate ACC greats Bobby Hurley and Sam Cassell, strong play from Evers Burns against future NBA foes Rodney Rogers and Matt Geiger, and energy from our freshmen Wayne Bristol and John Walsh to ignite the Terrapin machine. My teammates couldn't wait to battle against elite competitors each game day and the selflessness they demonstrated by pushing me to the front launches us beyond the multitude of challenges threatening to keep Maryland down. Statistics say the 1992 Maryland Terrapins team includes a player scoring at least thirty points in seven straight Atlantic Coast Conference games. I committed to playing my part, like all my teammates, sincerely.

The thirty-point streak gives the University of Maryland a few weeks of positive press to build on and before every interview I thought of Len Bias winning, giving interviews, and just being "The Man." Sitting at my locker inside Cole Field House for the last time as a Terrapin student-athlete, visualizing the flashpoints of the four-year journey, the tears pull me back to a time when basketball was just one of the games we played to fill the day. I reflected on the morning Len died, the day my life changed. I weighed the losses and the sanctions against the love and support of the Terrapin community and I know it's the awesome spirit of family in College Park that makes leaving hard to do.

Accepting the end of my Maryland career and removing the Terrapin jersey that blankets my heart creates an emotional volcano, and every memory brings more tears. I wiped my face with my jersey and realized how I had given blood, sweat, and tears to my Maryland and how the Terrapin Nation paid me back with friendship, loyalty, and pride. With that thought, I found the strength to close the locker room door on a character-shaping chapter and rejoin my waiting family. I hugged my mother and turned to see a group of fans lingering long after the final horn to say thanks, proud to support the Terrapin effort, and my sadness gave in to content. The affection we inspired started to spread and signaled the "all clear" to admit to the world once again that you were a Maryland fan. We succeeded giving everyone aboard Team Terp a reason to cheer. Before anyone feared the turtle, we needed to gain respect, a principal mission accomplished.

As the University raises my number forty-two beside the thirty-four jersey of the late Len Bias, I'm shivering with fulfillment as I think of my time in College Park and the incredible journey of the Maryland basketball program. In a flash, the mystic, farsighted vision from tenth grade of a nostalgic pause in Cole Field House resurfaces, and quickly fades once again.

I pictured the trusted local trio of incoming freshmen, Johnny Rhodes, Duane Simpkins and Exree Hipp, my boys, who were perfect complements to Coach Williams and would open more doors to the talent-rich "DMV." The torch-passing ceremony crosses my mind and I can't believe I'm living the ritual.

Flanked by my family, surveying Cole, cherishing the high-roofed home of Terp fans decked in Maryland gear, faces painted the school colors, screaming over the band for a local kid who only wanted to give Marylanders cause to celebrate College Park, my Maryland looked firm, and in good hands. We cleared a high hurdle.

Watching my jersey unfurl from the rafters, experiencing the bone-penetrating roar of an energetic Cole Field House with the emcee quantifying my commitment to Maryland, for one moment in time, I feel like "The Man," and I stand tall, thankful for having Len Bias to show me the way.

Choosing and sticking with Maryland mirrors the "Can-Do" attitude that runs through the basketball program and shapes the University. Hearing sportswriters portray the Terrapins as the worst team in the country united us, incited an all-out determination to achieve and compete, and pitted us against the world in our unrelenting drive to our rightful place. Every Terrapin who journeyed through one cruel moment after another with the untold strain from losing Len Bias gave us the fortitude to rise above labels and prove our worth. Those Maryland teams who played in the shadow of despair and heartache provided a framework for future Terrapins to right the platform, and regain national acceptance.

We are Maryland, proud of our past, climbing toward excellence.

The final game zips by in a blur, the crowd stands once more to celebrate the Terrapin Way, serenading our effort, and we fade into the tunnel of Cole Field House with new tags.

Student-athletes.

College basketball players.

Simply, the 1992 Maryland Terrapins.

We deserved the fundamental privilege.

We earned the title.

Throughout the community and around the region, talking Terps broadens smiles. The thirty-point streak soothed the complex wound with longed-for optimism and positive coverage for Maryland, the University of Maryland, and Maryland Basketball. Terrapin fans everywhere who tune in to catch sports on the radio and television seek and receive good news from College Park. Furthermore, the basketball nation and the casual sports enthusiast now have new reasons to understand something once uncertain: Maryland survives.

Team Terrapin toughness leads to a scattering of post-season acclamation and an invitation for me to attend the 1992 NBA pre-draft. However, attending class in order to graduate ranks number one on my must-do list. In the Walter, Sr. and Theresa Williams' household, a bachelor's degree from the University of Maryland trumps everything, including "The League."

After all, basketball opens only one lane on the expressway to a better life. The goal of becoming an NBA player from College Park began with my aspiration to excel as a student-athlete at Crossland High School. History and heartache demanded I graduate from the University of Maryland, to fulfill a privilege rather than an obligation, and to add a fresh spin on Prince George's County pride. Skipping classes and postponing a college degree to concentrate on basketball may work for some, but my parents watched me sign the letter of intent to attend the University of Maryland envisioning a scholarship in the traditional sense, meaning graduate into the workforce.

Keeping the spotlight on schoolwork leaves little time to listen to the media and its endless NBA lottery speculation. Wherever the draft leads, a degree from Maryland will pave my way to achieve. Attending class, clocking in at the gym, doing homework, knocking down extra jump shots, and preparing for finals consumes every second, but I could feel the love blooming in the "DMV."

Fielding a competitive basketball team and carving a slab of success enables the Terrapin Nation to rejoin the throng of proud sports fans. A thirty-second conversation with a group of students shouting "Go Terps" as we cross paths to and from class strengthens our unity. High-fives with the landscaping and maintenance crews extend our Terrapin family. Hearing words of encouragement from the drive-through window of a DC fast-food joint spreads the affection. Alumni walked taller, the University stood stronger, and strangers came together to speak a good word about Maryland Basketball and offer well-wishes for my future in "The League." College Park once again had the essence of intercollegiate sports: a strong and united community behind it. We represented all of Maryland, eagerly surfacing from the excruciating dark times.

The honor of having a positive effect on the recovery and renaissance of Maryland Basketball ranks highest among the many joys of my athletic life. Willingly drawn to College Park, proud of being Maryland, never wanting pity, we insisted on respect. We took on the immense pain and anguish caused by the loss of Len Bias and stopped it from spreading beyond the chip on our collective shoulder.

In effect, we never take off our Terp uniform; we can't. History will not allow us to disrobe from our unparalleled past.

We are Maryland. We are.

CHAPTER 8

"THE **LEAGUE**"

"One cruel moment doesn't have to break or define me."

TONY

In June of 1990, my NBA draft dream comes true. Coach Williams congratulates me and adds a smile of approval that's different from the looks of encouragement I received during the season. It has a touch of farewell. We looked back as we walked through the tunnel of Cole Field House, exchanging appreciation for sharing and contributing to what was for me a final voyage and for him an impressive opening season. Coach Williams acknowledged the advantages of having a senior captain at the helm of his storm-blown flagship and a commendable crew of fearless competitors to alleviate the uncertainty of our first year together.

I thanked Coach Williams for trusting the Terrapin Way.

Our discussion touches on life in the NBA with my new coach being a Tar Heel, a new Maryland legacy, and well-merited success. Coach Williams finishes by congratulating me on my ability to overcome adversity and emphasizes the commanding influence my graduating from Maryland into the NBA gives to College Park's forward momentum.

I understand the significance of a Terrapin graduating into "The League." Having one in our family "make it" is far more important than the "X's" and "O's," jump-hooks, and rebounds it took to get there. The basketball wisdom accumulated during the fight to reach the NBA may be valuable to the baby Terps and help them to become better student-athletes, but it's the path traveled to become a responsible adult and respected professional that means the most.

I remember shaking hands before exiting Cole, firmer than the coach-to-captain or father figure-to-son handshakes of times before. We walked through the "Field House" double doors together, two alumni, on our way to a better and brighter tomorrow.

Coach Williams succeeded reaching the Maryland in me, and I still hear him, loud and clear.

By rule and for the ferocious competition required to test my limits every day, I enlisted for the College Park training camp after a rookie year in the NBA, geared up to make personal strides in my performance and seasoned for my summer job tutoring Terps about next-level basketball. The work ethic developed through my lessons from Lenny lifted me into "The League" and the need to give back even a portion of what I've been given draws me home to empower the next generation.

Nabbing that familiar parking spot behind Cole Field House kick-starts my inaugural homecoming. My plan is to pop into the locker room and surprise the team with a box of NBA shirts and socks but Cole looks empty. Climbing the tortuous steps to the basketball office to see Coach Williams and the staff jogs memories of painful practice sessions and, as I reach for the doorknob, Walt walks out, on the way to play. The pickup games at "North Gym" start at noon and we need to hurry.

Life instantly returns to normal.

I volunteered to drive "this time," laughing all the way, reminiscing on futile efforts to find rides to the far side of campus. We cruised to "North Gym" in style, for once, but the struggle for prime parking never ends, especially now that a resurgent Maryland has raised the Eppley and Xfinity Centers.

The rhythmic ricochet of basketballs careening, shoes squeaking, and voices chiming one over the other rings like the best jazz in my ears. Walt and I turn the corner into "North Gym" and see the usual: both courts overflowing with the full spectrum from hopeful to professional.

This time, for the first time, the target is painted on my back: the NBA Player, one of the pros, recipient of each opponent's best shot, responsible for upholding a virtuous tradition, and looked to for leadership. More than that, I was a teammate of Lenny Bias who'd made it to the NBA. Excellent players like Keith Gatlin and Derrick Lewis were passed over in the tumult as it seemed the nation was determined to destroy us all because one of us fell to temptation. I believed that because of this, I had a duty to repay Maryland for all I had gained, and teach the new Terps not only the secrets of top-flight basketball, but also the hard-won lessons of grit and determination that I had learned with such pain.

I anticipated Walt, the new "Man" in College Park, battling with a heightened sense of purpose, hungry, and looking forward to measuring up against his teammate turned professional. Two minutes later, Walt dribbles baseline for the first basket of a new era, forcing me to take him to the low block and even the score, and the saga continued every summer for the duration of our playing careers, molding a legion of basketball players in the Terrapin Way.

Guarding "The Wizard" sharpens my perimeter defense and proves a first-rate preparation for defending the world-class small forwards in the NBA. Stellar Terps Derrick and Cedric Lewis pose unique technical challenges, driving me to refine and develop effective "in the paint" skills essential against the varying types of big men patrolling "The League." Jerrod Mustaf raises the bar each day, displaying NBA first-round draft-worthiness, and all-around talent. The passionate intra-squad tangles and the unpredictable rotation of battles against the best of the "DMV" benefit everyone. At the end of the day, when play turns to conversation, I delivered simple and straight-shooting messages.

Learn from Lenny.

Make the most of your talents at every stage of development.

In the end, the reward is in how we represent Maryland and the game.

WALT

Receiving the certified invitation to attend the 1992 NBA draft ceremony stimulates the jitters. Successfully disregarding the pre-draft projections helps me stay in the moment and enjoy chasing the dream but the special request to make an appearance brings anxiety. I need a suit in case NBA Commissioner David Stern calls me up to shake my hand.

In a far more important sense, I need to dress appropriately if I'm to stand in the footsteps of "The Man." Thinking of being drafted without reflecting on Len Bias is simply impossible. Len's life shaped the path that brought me to this moment, both by inspiring my play and scaring me straight. Staring at the NBA seal on the official letter signifying this definitive athletic milestone, I accept my fate. I will play in "The League" because a teenage kid from Crossland High School needed a way to ease his pain, the pain of losing "The Man."

The 1992 NBA draft takes place in Portland, Oregon. My body is there, but my spirit lingers in a Maryland hospital room with my ailing father. After acing the auditions for franchises interested in my service, especially the Denver Nuggets, I canceled the final pre-draft workout to spend time with Dad. My family comes to a consensus: Dad can't fly cross-country regardless of how much he wants to attend the draft.

My instant reaction is to cancel the trip. I don't need to be at the draft as much as I need to be with my family.

Without my parents at the table when my name is called, the ceremony will only remind me of what's missing. This success, above all things, belongs to my family, who sacrificed, nurtured, and supported my long climb to the pros. Kissing my mother on her cheek as she shines in the spotlight, hugging my sister who dared me to be somebody, and a quiet word with my father before I step on stage is all that really matters. The time-honored handshake with the NBA Commissioner just adds a nice cap to the ceremony.

The suggestion to fly alone out to Oregon and return immediately after the draft sounds completely unappealing. I'd rather answer the call from the hospital telephone right next to "Pops." The emotional rollercoaster shakes me up. An NBA future excites me one second and for the next fifty-nine, I'm gripped by an incapacitating fear that my one true hero won't be with me for the ride. We discussed the options, my father explained what I needed to do, and my numb body boarded an airplane to the Pacific Northwest.

The executives from the Sacramento Kings asked more questions, and more intrusive questions, than any of the other franchises. No one actually mentions Len Bias but the occasional references to drug use during the day-long scrutiny with the Sacramento brass confirms what I feared. Decision-makers within the 1992 National Basketball Association are still stuck in a "College Park 1986" state of mind.

Sacramento elects to dig deepest, going so far as to question the morality of the average Prince George's County citizen, and placing my community on trial six years beyond reason. The Sacramento interrogation proves that the vile public image of Maryland basketball players is alive and well and we still stand tattooed with a scarlet letter, just as it was when the doors wouldn't open for Terps Keith Gatlin and Derrick Lewis.

Unwilling to accept that this inquisition was routine NBA procedure, I resented the extended inspection. In hindsight, the pointed questioning signaled that the Kings had a genuine interest. Sacramento needed a small forward and I offered an attractive option but the shocking death of Len Bias altered the perception of high-profile student-athletes, Maryland basketball players above all. Consequently, the Kings scheduled a thorough examination: a two-hour on-court workout, an "X" and "O" session with the coaches, a sit-down with team owner Jim Thomas, a written evaluation, a late lunch grilling by staff members, and a one-on-one dinner conversation with head coach Gary St. Jean. At the end, I walked back to my hotel room with mixed feelings: confident the Kings value my small forward skill set but equally disenchanted by the unfairness of the protracted audition.

Sacramento: Not likely.

Early in the morning on draft day, the Philadelphia 76ers telephone to say they want me and plan on using their ninth pick of the first round to show me some brotherly love. I freeze, head in hand, imagining being drafted onto cloud number nine. Philadelphia: only two hours from home, family and friends in the stands for every home game, "Dr. J," Maurice Cheeks, and my moment on stage with NBA Commissioner David Stern.

This glorious vision quickly evaporates, overtaken by an eerie memory of a smiling Len Bias on his draft day. Maryland and Massenburg come to mind, and I remember the joy of Len joining the World Champion Boston Celtics melting away two days later. Doubters who cannot see past the cruel cosmic irony will question investing in another player from Prince George's County. The well-wishers in and around Maryland may watch the 1992 draft to cheer for the local kid but, in the back of their minds, they remember Len Bias and wonder if fate might lead the latest Terrapin draftee down a similar self-destructive path.

The discovery of a true suitor in Philadelphia provides relief. The 76ers. Me, a first-round draft pick of the fabulous Philadelphia 76ers, a Crossland kid soon to talk hoops with "The Doctor." The image of "Dr. J" dunking in a white lab coat morphs into the doctors busy caring for my father, and all else is forgotten.

On the draft day bus ride to the arena, the carousel of thoughts spinning in my head centers on following in the footsteps of Len Bias, from the blacktop through the mud to the doorstep of fame, trusting that everything my Maryland has taught makes me ready for life in "The League." The bus stops and the possibility of Philadelphia trading the ninth pick jumps into my mind like an oversized, bold-print question mark. I could end up anywhere, but I'm good to go.

Conscious of the grace that got me here, I thank God for the blessings. On the basketball court and in the game of life, the primal urge to achieve and the fortitude to bear hardships on the road to success often distinguish the great from the good. Striving to be like Len Bias, a Maryland great, required unusual endurance but the prize has been worth the struggle. I marched a sanctified path into Portland Memorial Coliseum on draft day with Terrapin shoulders high, thoroughly tested, prepared, and ready to represent Prince George's County, Maryland on the world stage.

No one anticipates the heartbreak when a seventeen-year-old walks on air to the University of Maryland, privileged and pumped up to learn from Lenny and "Lefty," believing College Park is the launching pad to the NBA, only to plunge into years of persecution and pain. Reaching for "The League" through the

shadows of the cruelest moment has resulted in the education of a lifetime.

The lessons of survival cemented at the University of Maryland have discipline at the core, the most important skill for evolving to meet the demands of an NBA on the rise, and a personal life in transition. Having to learn and adapt to the teaching styles of three head coaches within a five-year period could have easily stunted the development of a student-athlete, but the experience toughened me and made me more versatile, and the attitude that comes from constantly adapting leads me through the roadblocks.

Changing teams and cities in twenty-four hours unleashes an ambush of challenges. How a player handles such a move will affect his subsequent playing time, and eventually, his earning potential. Every new management team combines high expectations with slim regard for personal issues.

To them, only performance matters.

Without the leverage of a long-term deal, or a few weeks to learn the system, needing to exit the airplane ready to play becomes my only NBA option. Life in "The League" on one-year contracts means constant auditioning, standard operating procedure in the "get the job done" philosophy that shaped the student-athletes at Maryland. Outlasting and thriving beyond the darkness that came with losing Lenny dwarfs anything the NBA can dish out. A hard-charging work ethic enhanced by studying "The Man" and the will of a survivor from being a Terrapin under water provides an abundance of the resolve needed to keep grinding.

For me and my family, slipping into the second-round of the 1990 NBA draft, the forty-third pick, prompts joyous embraces rather than frustrated grimaces. We understood that the NBA owes prospective employees nothing, so we celebrated the moment of recognition as a remarkable occurrence. Suffering through the harshest example of the promise that there are no guarantees in life except death taught us to rejoice in the moment: a college graduate rewarded with a chance to earn a

living playing the backyard game he loves. That's a win in anyone's book.

Being released from an NBA team and fighting to win a spot with another franchise would test the mettle of even the best-conditioned among us. The toll on mind and body required to remain employed in this quick-change version of the NBA taxes every fiber but can't compare to the constant strain of pressing through agony after the death of my friend and teammate.

Innocence and a gradual introduction to real-world issues is supposed to be the charm of college, the so-called time of your life, but for the 1986 University of Maryland student-athlete, comfort vanished overnight. The real world struck John Johnson, Dave Dickerson, Greg Nared, and me with near-lethal force. I was eighteen trying to overcome personal misery and public condemnation in order to work past an unforgettable tragedy. If an evil professor were to design a program to teach endurance and eternal perseverance, playing basketball at Maryland in the late 80's would be central to the curriculum. The problems of a life in pro basketball aren't even in the same league.

The 1992 NBA draft class received recognition as a top collection of basketball talent with future Hall of Fame members Shaquille O'Neal from Louisiana State University, Alonzo Mourning from Georgetown, and Christian Laettner from Duke; the consensus number one, two, and three picks, respectively. The Dallas Mavericks selected fourth and the butterflies in my belly started to flap.

Dallas chooses Jimmy Jackson, my Pan Am Games teammate and star recruit for Coach Williams at Ohio State University. The Denver Nuggets owned the rights to the fifth pick and I remembered the good times in Colorado shooting to win a medal for the USA, flourishing during an individual workout with the Nuggets, and I see images of Denver great Alex English. Maybe Denver, Colorado will become my new DC. The pulse in my neck beats against my collar as the clock ticks for

Denver. Only the echoes of promise from the pre-draft conversation with Philadelphia in concert with the advantages of playing close to home on the East Coast tames my tension. Commissioner Stern moves toward the podium to strike the pose and reveal the fifth selection.

The Denver Nuggets opt for LaPhonso Ellis from Notre Dame leaving me with a bitter taste of disappointment. Worrying about something totally beyond my control breaks a golden rule, so I let it go. The Nuggets took "The Phons," and I started to think about Richie Cunningham, Arthur Fonzarelli, and the "Happy Days" tune, and with that song in my head, it was easier to think positively.

My sports agent, Terrapin legend and Atlantic Coast Conference all-time great Len Elmore, discovered early on draft day that my lucky number will be seven: Sacramento has targeted me as its next King. Mr. Elmore, aiming to preserve the element of surprise, answers every call and question with a cool poker face, leaving me to suffer through a guessing game with picks six, seven, and eight, looking around the room at the other players, and wondering who will go where.

My boyhood favorites, the Washington Bullets choose sixth. My friends and family trusted with complete confidence that the DC brain trust would use pick six to select their native son. This neighborhood partiality resulted from wishful thinking but being "The Wizard" in Washington sounds good and the prospect of playing NBA basketball minutes from home gives me a "this is it" feeling. The Bullets, however, had not requested an individual workout, an alarming decision the locals defended by saying there was no need for a supplementary analysis considering my four-year exhibition just up Route One in Cole Field House. Fans place great value on loyalty and devotion to home—NBA owners and general managers, far less.

With hope raining possibilities on draft day, becoming a Washington Bullet seems Hollywood and too wonderful to want. I thought maybe Denver, possibly Philadelphia, but never the Bullets, until the Commissioner approaches the podium to announce the Washington pick. A dark blue number forty-two Bullets jersey waves before my eyes, with the red and white stripes across the front like the classic number forty-one made famous by Hall of Fame Champion Wes Unseld. Commissioner Stern stands before the microphone and I see a Terp Nation convoy on

Interstate 95 with my friends and family able to witness the hometown kid help Pervis Ellison and Michael Adams make the Bullets a better team. The silence at our table triples the shivers.

"And with the sixth pick," Washington chooses a versatile forward from the ACC, Tom Gugliotta. The Washington Bullets, a team with its home arena in Prince George's County, passes over a versatile, ACC forward from right next door. Bewilderment runs its course. I settle on the Bullets opting for Gugliotta's post game over my perimeter skills and turn the focus to images of Rocky Balboa on the steps in Philadelphia.

Slanting in my chair breathing out concern, worrying about my Dad, uncertain if watching this process from a hospital bed lifts or saddens him, I realize one sure thing about the Bullets decision: my father will curse Coach Unseld forever.

The clock ticks as I digest the hometown letdown and with pick number seven, the Sacramento Kings select, "…from the University of Maryland."

Stunned!

With DC on my mind and Sacramento far from it, I never considered being chosen seventh. The Kings? I hesitated to stand, unable to fully absorb the euphoria of instant discovery, but the loving look on my mother's face told me it was indeed our time. I kissed her, hugged my sister and my niece, and I felt my father getting up from the table to meet me in the aisle, looking at the boy he made, arms open wide. I heard him say, "Son," and his voice echoed above the applause like his words have all my life. I could see him standing there, and I whispered to him, "Thanks, Dad."

The attendant gives me the ceremonial hat, the revolutionary Commissioner David Stern shakes my hand, we pause for pictures, the cameras flash, and the magical moment ends.

Another team receives notice of being "on the clock."

Tilting my NBA cap slightly to the side in tribute to Len Bias, I exited stage left a Terrapin King. The lights dimmed, and before being whisked away to greet my new bosses, I removed the ceremonial hat to admire the crowning symbol of achievement, my reward for following the path. Entranced by the team logo, my eyes lock onto the words "men" and "to" flashing within SACRAMENTO and the image stirs somber reminders of the two men most responsible for the momentous occasion being noticeably absent.

My father should have been beaming beside me and Len Bias should have been watching from anywhere in the world, both boasting, "That's my boy."

Bittersweet.

Playing for twelve NBA teams over fifteen years of professional basketball often leads to lively conversations about the highs and lows of a nomadic career. Playing basketball for a living is a privilege. The journey is the process.

Achieving success "on the move" requires a versatile skill set, one in demand regardless of the team dynamic or its executive philosophy. The ability to quickly adjust to circumstances remains an asset in "The League," a talent I mastered while playing for three head coaches during the aftermath of the heartbreak at Maryland. Where some NBA players who get traded to a new squad struggle to retain the skills that brought them to the elite level, change did not sway my resolution, reduce my productivity, or diminish my aggressive style of play. I adopted a tried-and-true approach to surviving the rigors of the NBA: show my best every day.

Managing the stress associated with fitting into a new scheme once or even twice in a single season can prevent an athlete from finding a groove and leave him wandering far outside the zone. I avoided morphing into a system-dependent player by understanding, accepting, and besting expectations. The rhythm never skips a beat when you're prepared.

Summers at Maryland studying "North Gym 101" give me a leg up on the competition entering pre-season training camps and I cannot imagine a player or coach who is mentally tougher. The lessons from Lenny point toward success regardless of the situation. "The Man from Landover" left me well-equipped to

handle the ebb and flow of life because the journey beyond a shooting star requires determination etched in stone.

Wearing NBA jerseys representing cities from Massachusetts to California and both Canadian franchises gives me a greater appreciation for the blessing with every new team. Being number thirty-four for the San Antonio Spurs provided the spiritual advantage I needed to win a fifteenth season against Father Time.

A few days before winning the 2005 NBA Championship with the Spurs, I read an article in the Houston Chronicle written by John P. Lopez that nearly brought tears to my eyes. In one sentence, Mr. Lopez summed up everything I had been feeling for twenty years. One cruel moment doesn't have to break me or define me. I thought about those words as I sat in the championship locker room shortly after winning the title, and as a media photographer showed me the picture he'd just snapped of me posing with the Larry O'Brien Championship Trophy, my eyes focused on the number thirty-four radiating in the lights reflecting onto my uniform. At that moment, I decided to never wear Lenny's number again.

Unimaginably, a severe ankle injury from a car accident two months later ends my career, but the last photograph of me as an NBA player shows me wearing the number thirty-four, a championship picture. I can now accept it as a fulfilling homage to "The Man."

I followed Lenny to Maryland in the summer of 1985 to live the dream of teaming up with my idol and exactly two decades later, I arrived at an NBA championship, the apex of professional basketball, accomplishing a seemingly impossible goal.

In between, I lived to overcome.

Staying the course, facing the insurmountable obstacles, and battling the giants of basketball for fifteen years lead to a World Champion title and, at the end of my time on the court, I get to ride in a parade along the San Antonio River Walk and feel a sense of closure, permitting the acceptance of the inevitable.

Number thirty-four retires on top.

The pilot dips the wing during descent and gives me a first look at the landscape of Sacramento, California, my new home on the West Coast. What looks like a mound on an open range turns into a herd of grazing cattle crudely spelling out the phrase "FAR FROM DC." The tree-lined rural setting is a one-hundred-and-eighty-degree shift from Temple Hills, Maryland and causes a hiccup of anxiety. The thrill of landing in the capital of California to play basketball with the best makes everything all right.

Driving toward the arena for the first meet and greet with the Sacramento community, I drifted back to June 18, 1986, imagining "The Man" rolling through Boston, living the dream that divine day. Following Len Bias to Maryland paved the earliest steps of the path. I needed to succeed as a King to complete the example for the next Prince George's County youngster. The car slows during a brief tour of downtown Sacramento and, like a magnet attracting my attention, a man wearing a Hoyas shirt standing like a statue with both hands to the sky cuts through the crowd. While lowering the window to raise a fist and recognize the shout out from the "DMV," memories of how I considered transferring to Georgetown after the NCAA sanctioned Maryland Basketball pop into my mind. The family drive to see me play would have been even shorter than the swift thirty-minute trip to College Park. The reflection floodgates reopen and I imagine what life might have been like if I'd left Maryland to chase a championship at UNLV or Villanova. The enthusiastic fans of Sacramento forming a curbside welcome committee reinforced a truth: Nothing Tops Being a King.

Except, perhaps, being from the University of Maryland.

Having a beloved uncle die young caused me to make a sharp withdrawal from friends and take a deep dive into unhappiness. Len Bias died shortly thereafter and I turned single-mindedly toward a lonely search for basketball excellence. At the University of Maryland, absorbing grief and criticism thickened my skin, and the "us against the world" attitude our team adopted forms a shield for my suffering psyche. Twenty-four days before playing in my first NBA game, Walter Williams, Sr. lost his fight against cancer, and the emptiness that takes over after losing my Dad, my partner, leaves me transparently hollow and the total withdrawal process becomes complete.

The veterans on the 1992-1993 Sacramento squad supported me and my family like lifelong blood brothers even though circumstances prevented me from attending a single pre-season practice. The unexpected response of my Sacramento teammates exemplifies the bonding power of a good team, an instant brotherhood. The cast of Kings showing compassion for my pain makes me want to recover. Beyond basketball, their conduct during my crisis parallels the Good Samaritan taking care of the wounded rookie alone on the road. My guy Anthony Bonner, Hall of Fame Champion Mitch Richmond, three-time Champion Randy Brown, College Hall of Fame stars Lionel Simmons and Wayman Tisdale, 1986 NBA Slam Dunk Champion Anthony "Spud" Webb, and all the rest of that squad of first-class gentlemen sheltered and guided me through the most difficult time of my life. The Sacramento basketball family covered me with a West Coast version of brotherly love, a capital permit to thrive, and a much-needed blessing.

With the benefit of an empathetic new team and communities on both coasts sustaining my family and me, the time arrives for the unforgettable first taste of NBA action, a pre-season match against the World Champion Chicago Bulls. With the ball in my hands and the tension of an expiring shot clock, the incomparable Michael Jordan switches from defending Mitch Richmond to guarding me as All-Defensive First-Team and 2010 Hall of Fame swingman Scottie Pippen skates from me to shadow Mitch. The wily maneuver provides me the eagerly anticipated opportunity to go one-on-one against the greatest player in "The League" and score a basket before the buzzer sounds. Completely cognizant of challenging a world-class defender, I initiate the long-planned footwork necessary to set up the NBA MVP for a signature crossover dribble. The exaggerated shoulder lean causes the desired shift in defender balance, the proven indicator to execute a move perfected through a decade of success against elite competition. As the ball slides down my fingers, I realize there's trouble, but too late. Jordan plucks the ball away, retrieves it, flashes down court, and slams it through for an easy two.

The game took place in Toronto, Canada but the crowd goes so crazy you'd have thought they flew in from Chicago. Michael Jordan gallops past me with a big grin, taps me on the backside, and says, "We watch film up here at this level."

That's Championship Schooling from day one with nowhere to go but up.

Our 1992 draft class formed an immediate and lasting impact on the NBA with twenty-three seasoned college seniors selected in the first round, and four juniors including the unstoppable Shaquille O'Neal. No sophomores. No freshmen. No one from high school. In our day, first-round draft picks needed to contribute; potential stayed in college. Most of the 1992 first-round draftees earned the option to forfeit college eligibility for an early start in "The League" but NBA owners and general managers preferred the experienced over the "works in progress." Lottery-pick expectations demanded instant NBA-caliber production and we entered "The League" primed, vowing at our rookie symposium to validate being ranked among the deepest NBA drafts by leaving an indelible mark. Daily glimpses at the box scores and biweekly battles against classmates served as fraternal motivation for excellence and achievement.

On the second day of January 1993, I led the way for Sacramento with forty points against the Philadelphia 76ers to get my name in the newspaper and become the first of the 1992 class to hit the memorable scoring mark. In our locker room after the game, my team of Kings delivered a rousing serenade with a most familiar chorus: "We're off to see the Wizard."

Wonderful.

Lenny Bias pushes me every day. From the time he blossomed into a super sophomore in 1983, through my final moments on an NBA court, and as I live today, Lenny serves as my reason to never give up the fight and to always do more than expected.

He taught me, Dave Dickerson, Greg Nared, and John Johnson how to work on the court, in the weight room, and through the playbook to transform raw talent into a professional athlete, while definitively proving to all the absolute power of consequence. We landed in College Park true freshmen, gifted to some

degree with a talent for basketball, in awe of "The Man" like every wannabe ball player.

Lenny knew we admired, looked up to, and imagined being like him but the warm spotlight of our adulation never changed him. He was determined to show us greatness. He loved being a Maryland Terrapin and demanded we personify the Turtle as well. And since he practiced every drill like a championship was on the line, so did we, the only way to play basketball when being the best is the goal.

On occasion, Coach Driesell needed to remove Lenny from the court during practice so the rest of the team could run a play without his dominating presence. Lenny did it all for his Terrapins, permitting us to play our first year of ACC basketball with a rare and supreme confidence: We could win against anyone.

Lenny left a convincing blueprint and his passion for excellence is a signature trait I constantly strive to develop. My efforts to emulate "The Man" turned into a well-regarded quality and allowed me to remain a valuable commodity in the minds of NBA coaches and general managers until I retired. I lean on that quality to live. The lessons from Lenny teach us to be better than the moment.

Choosing to leave the NBA behind and accept a guaranteed contract to test the best of Europe during the 1993 season was one of the most difficult professional decisions I faced in pro basketball. A five-star performance as a free agent on the NBA summer circuit persuades several teams to extend training camp invitations, but an invitation is a low-odds gamble when the team doesn't have the confidence to seal it with a guarantee.

Saying goodbye to "The League" and closing a door that may never reopen is a calculated risk. I kept pace with the Hall of Fame "Admiral" David Robinson and Antoine "Big Dawg" Carr, letting me know I could succeed in the States at the highest level. NBA coaches whispering sweet nothings every week of the summer added to my optimism. Earning an October roster spot seemed certain.

These daydreams were pleasant but they didn't even compare

to the fact that back in San Antonio, my son was about to be born, and every day without a binding contract jeopardized his future. To make the move across the ocean a temporary detour, I had to dominate the European courts and earn a one-way ticket back home. European basketball presented an attractive alternative and grew into a super league, and I planned to cross the pond again, but only on vacation after doing everything necessary to remain an active member of the National Basketball Association.

A representative of the Los Angeles Clippers has an eye on me at the 1993-94 Euro-All Star game, and after epic battles with seven-feet-three, three-hundred-pound Hall of Fame giant Arvydas Sabonis and two Spanish League championships, the Clippers offer a two-year deal to play in L.A. The NBA logo jumps into my head and my subconscious screams the familiar "Where do I sign?" Accepting the NBA challenge required an occasional late-night wrestling match with "The Mailman" Karl Malone followed by a matinee clash with Superman himself, Shaquille O'Neal, two of the most powerful low-post players in the Hall of Fame. Sizeable obligations, but I did it.

I learned to handle anything.

The life and times of Tony Massenburg has all the hallmarks of classic theater. The leading man grows up in rural Virginia dreaming of becoming an NBA player, earns a scholarship to play alongside his idol, spends one season on a rock star tour learning from the greatest, at eighteen suffers the tragic loss of his friend, teammate, and role model, endures the mayhem of playing for three college coaches and, conquering all the trials and tribulations, plays for twelve NBA teams in fifteen seasons and retires as a World Champion with the team that originally drafted him.

No matter who writes the screenplay, the last credit will read, "Directed by Len Bias."

My parents passed down a hard-nosed determination.

A love of basketball and the motivating drive to emulate number thirty-four from Maryland, to team with "The Man," made College Park my only destination. A summer of pickup games and six weeks of pre-season scrimmages with Lenny turned two precious hopes into realities: Bias was "The Man," and he was willing to teach me the invaluable keys to his athletic proficiency.

Lenny giving maximum effort during every practice showed me what to do with the fire in my belly. Being beat down by Bias during five-day winless spells and scrapping to offer resistance worthy of his respect built the framework I would need to secure an unpredictable future. I learned above all to persevere and that is what forms the foundation of my skill set as an athlete and is the solid base from which I have ventured beyond basketball.

With perspective, obstacles are only preludes to achievement like hurdles on the winding path to an NBA championship, proving that the right attitude will change you for the better, and then you can change your future. Overcoming the complications of a mid-season trade or the livelihood-threatening uncertainty of a ten-day contract seems achievable to a "Master of Radical Transformation." To balance on the NBA carousel, I delivered a constructive impact, from the front office to the locker room, proving daily that I was worthy of staying in the rotation.

Anyone fighting the daily crush of a perform-or-else workplace understands the potential to be overwhelmed but the great depression of College Park formed a natural, cerebral barrier that protected survivors from collapsing under even the worst-case scenarios.

We have a tough external shell; we're Terrapins.

The first and perhaps only option for enduring and conquering hardship begins with giving maximum effort. Knowing I can devote everything it takes makes the turbulence of a globe-trotting basketball adventure a dream I can manage.

Chapter 9

TERRAPIN **PRIDE**

"I knew very little about the ACC until Maryland started recruiting me but I remember hearing of this guy who could have been better than Michael Jordan. The situation seemed unfortunate but Maryland being a big enough program to have a great player such as Len Bias wanting to go there was interesting and attractive, and elevated Maryland in my mind.

Visiting College Park, seeing Tony and Walt in the NBA succeeding at the highest level, learning their journey and the struggle to keep Maryland strong, following Steve Francis, the best player in college, teaming with Juan Dixon and talking with them about overcoming adversity, I was surrounded by inspiration. I fell in love with the program, the people who kept Maryland great."

—Steve Blake, NCAA Champion, NBA Record Holder, Terrapin Legend

TONY

Pride comes from affirmation. Seven freshmen chose Maryland in 1985, five frontcourt players, Greg Nared, and John Johnson, one of the best guards in the country, with a vision of how being a teammate of the ACC Player of the Year impacts the future. I saw Lenny leading us to a national championship, and I planned to study his excellence every second we spent together.

My first notes were on his intensity. "The Man" came out of

the gate on fire. He said, "That's how Terrapins play." During games, he talked constantly and unapologetically: on defense, to the other team, to the referees, and to anyone else who needed to hear us coming. We were second to no one, and I loved feeling like a top dog, the favorites, playing beside the best player in college. Off the court, Lenny was an easygoing megastar. I knew this, but when we landed in Hawaii for my first tournament experience, I saw crowds gathering as if a king had just arrived.

Prior to coming to College Park, Lenny was my star, my idol, "The Man" for Maryland. I assumed everybody had heard of Lenny Bias, but I loved everything about him. On the beaches of Hawaii, I recognized that Lenny had a nationwide following who also believed he walked on water. Most of the people on the island only knew of the University of Maryland because of Lenny Bias, but he put us in front.

He talked about how hard the freshmen were working to push the upperclassmen, how Derrick Lewis was going to be a force, how Keith Gatlin was the best point guard in college basketball, how thankful we were for the veterans of Pearl Harbor, and how proud we were to represent Maryland out west. He was a genuine statesman, signing every autograph with a gracious smile, and he was a big, lovable college kid, playing catch on the beach with strangers and crashing into the ocean waves. Everybody loved Lenny Bias and he loved everyone until game time. That's how Terrapins are.

Lenny dominated the Hawaii tournament and made sure that anyone on the island who hears about Maryland sees red and thinks Bias. He scored twenty tough points in a double-overtime clash with Stanford and twenty-nine points with ten rebounds in the championship victory over host Hawaii Pacific. As we celebrated, I joined the chorus screaming, "You're The Man, Lenny," and he turned to me and said, "You're next."

I believed him. I felt ready.

Our next game was the first game of the ACC season, a home game against the star-spangled Duke Blue Devils and Coach Driesell put me in the starting lineup, another part of the dream coming true. In less than seven months, I went from a rural Virginia high school athlete to starting alongside my idol in a sold-out Cole Field House. Lenny wouldn't let me be nervous; he said it's where I belong. We banged against future NBA first-round picks Danny Ferry and Mark Alarie and a cast of future pros, and "The Man" scored twenty-eight points to set the tone for how we needed to attack every team in the ACC. Lenny poured in forty-one points the next time we faced the second-ranked Blue Devils and, less than a month later, he put on a show against number-one North Carolina that some call one of the greatest performances in the history of college basketball.

Before falling in love with Lenny Bias, I rooted for the Tar Heels. My high school coach, Ralph Joyner, a huge Dean Smith and Tar Heel fan, wanted to run the Carolina system and packed us into a van for annual trips to Chapel Hill to watch the team work out and learn from the best. We walked around Carmichael Arena in awe, looking in on a big-time college practice, watching the great Dean Smith orchestrate Mike Jordan's acrobatics, James Worthy's combination of power and quickness, and Sam Perkins' smoothness at six-feet-nine-inches tall. Every move was so precise: the timing on their screen-setting, the footwork, the spacing, the teamwork. They sprinted from station to station without a wasted moment. It was art and I went home more amazed at Coach Smith than the players because his organization created superstars. Then Lenny Bias jumped into the scene.

The February 1986 game against North Carolina was a must-win for us, our last chance to avenge a series of heartbreaking losses to the Tar Heels, but it wasn't just Maryland versus Carolina. It was "The Left-Hander" against "The Dean of Basketball." The nation's number one team versus the number one player. Old School Cole Field House against the brand new "Dean Dome."

The "Dean Dome" looked majestic as we pulled into the parking lot but we could see in Lenny's eyes that he was approaching this game like a war. He said beating the best makes us the best and sends that message to the world. We walked in knowing Lenny gave us a chance to make history and be the first team to beat the Tar Heels in their new building, and we believed Coach Driesell deserved that distinction. Warming up in the sparkling, fancy, modern arena with twenty-two thousand fans looking on made me feel like a pro, but when the public-address announcer called my name to enter the game, I forgot who Coach Driesell said to go in for. I just looked to Lenny and he told me what to do.

There was an extra buzz inside the arena because of the made-for-television matchup between possible number one draft picks Brad Daugherty and Lenny Bias. Every possession felt like it could be the deciding factor and we needed everyone's best effort along with a superhuman performance from "The Man" to beat the "Baby Blues."

The game was close throughout until the Tar Heels took a nine-point lead with less than three minutes left. Coach Driesell called a time out and while the staff talked strategy, Lenny took over the huddle.

He said, "We're winning this game," and the next series of plays showed the world that Lenny Bias was the most dominant and complete player in college basketball. About five seconds after we inbounded the ball, Lenny caught a pass and knocked down a signature, nothing-but-net, jump shot from just in front of our bench. Two seconds later, he stole their inbound pass and elevated over six-feet-eleven Warren Martin for a backwards, two-handed dunk that will live forever. We scored six points in fifty seconds, forcing North Carolina to call a time out, and we knew they were rattled. Lenny blocked the next Tar Heel shot, grabbed the next rebound, and with less than a minute left in regulation, hit a top-of-the-key jumper to cut their lead to two. Jeff Baxter nailed a clutch jump shot to tie the game at the end of regulation and we'd come from way behind to power into overtime with all the momentum.

The extra five minutes flew by. Lenny hit a big-time shot in traffic to give us a one-point lead and with fifteen seconds left, he swatted Kenny Smith's potential game-winning layup to knock the Tar Heels from their lofty perch. When Keith Gatlin tricked

everyone by bouncing the ball off Kenny Smith's back for the victory-sealing basket, I exploded off the bench like a rocket.

Lenny Bias scores a remarkable thirty-five points against the number one blue bloods on prime-time television, Maryland wins, Terrapin pride spreads nationwide, and College Park shines like "The Capital of College Basketball."

We were on top of the world.

WALT

Sacramento drafting Evers Burns in 1993 reaffirms the rising status of Terrapin Basketball, and we celebrated being the Kings from College Park by cross-checking our connections in search of Beltway chitchat about the heavily anticipated, cross-town showdown: Powerhouse Georgetown versus Mysterious Maryland.

I listened with one ear to my cousin in DC predicting the nationally televised butt-whipping his Hoyas would surely deliver to my "Turtles." Before attempting to interject a Terrapin rebuttal, thoughts of NCAA sanctions interrupted. Hearing "Terps" and "live television" immediately followed by sanctions for two years makes Maryland Basketball on prime time, nationwide, holiday weekend television hard to believe. It brings a temporary halt to the Hoya noise, and then my cousin screaming into the telephone snaps me back to the future. I added a humble opinion: The youngsters from College Park, my boys, were set to make a statement, red and ready for this confrontation, this moment. My cousin deserved the last word, respecting the national ranking of his Hoyas, but I ended with a warning, "Watch out for the new kid, Joe Smith."

In typical Georgetown fashion, my cousin shouts, "Joe who? Joe Schmoe." He jokes about the plain name and finishes with a profanity-laced round of anti-Terrapin observations.

The sound of other family members in the background talking up the Terps makes me miss Maryland and the give-and-take family smack talk so representative of a great hometown rivalry. Georgetown playing Maryland makes in-house archenemies break into an animated soundtrack worthy of a Michael Buffer introduction. Two storied basketball programs traveling on the same road in different directions, separated by a short car ride but they're a world apart. The capital neighborhood battle will finally take place again, with monumental consequences.

We hosted the Houston Rockets on the same night as the big Maryland versus Georgetown game, one day after an uplifting Thanksgiving with relatives from Maryland in town for the holiday. With six former ACC players on our roster, the chatter during the morning practice turned into a team-wide Talk-Terp session. I provided a P.G. County perspective on the regional significance of beating Georgetown and Evers spoke from his Baltimore roots. Both points of view led us beyond the on-court conflict to the "springboard effect."

A nationally televised win over the local giant would validate the resurgence of Maryland Basketball, open recruiting doors, and ignite a culture shift in the "DMV." Evers vouched for Keith Booth as "B-more" tough, a certified "baller" from the opening tip. We hit on the strengths of our dynamic trio from the DC area—Johnny Rhodes, Exree Hipp, and Duane Simpkins—each an A-student in "North Gym 101," supremely energized by the once-in-a-lifetime chance to represent and well-prepared for the elite challenge. No one anticipated Joe Smith flashing the brilliance of a future Naismith Award winner in his first college game. Stars formed, with bright lights emanating from the Capital Centre in Landover, Maryland, home of "The Man," shining on College Park once again.

Scanning the radio for college basketball news during the drive toward downtown Sacramento to face the Rockets and hearing nothing on the Terps worries me. It's a big game; somebody should be talking about it, especially if the Terps won. I rolled into ARCO Arena speeding through pleasantries, dashing straight for the television in the lounge to find Evers standing beside the screen, smiling. A news crew is talking sports. Twenty seconds into the report, the sports anchor turns to look directly at Evers and me and says, "And in college basketball, an upset."

Our shoulder-bumps and high-fives last longer than the few clips of highlights, but we clearly hear the anchor proclaim, "He's no ordinary Joe." My cousin blurting the "Joe who" comment comes to mind and I imagine the DC Friday night hot spots filled with more Terp fans than ever, talking about my boys. I expected the establishments on "The Route" in College Park to rock the whole weekend. I heard they did.

Maryland laughs last.

The 1993 triumph over Georgetown places Maryland one up in the neighborhood and squarely in the national discussion again, this time for winning. Nonetheless, my greatest pleasure from the crowning achievement derives from my affection for our fabulous five Terrapins. Exree Hipp, Duane Simpkins, and Johnny Rhodes uniting to rebuild my Maryland cannot be overstated. Their momentous commitment attracted the perfect pair, legends Keith Booth and Joe Smith, elevating the Terps to Kings of the Nation's Capital and founders of a new era of Maryland Basketball. My boys.

To soothe the sting of the Friday night loss to Houston, I surfed the sports news channels looking for "Terrapins topple Hoyas" highlights. Watching the instant classic, game-winning basket by Simpkins made me remember his development during the influential summer pickup sessions on campus. Simpkins coming through in the clutch is the magnificent merger of talent, will, and a deft application of the indispensable lessons learned in "North Gym."

After an exhausting day of rumbling for recognition and understanding inside the hot-house gymnasium, only the frustrated few rushed to exit the building. Lingering and letting the cool-down chats solidify the tutorial yields inside knowledge too valuable to miss. The Terps and the high-flying flock of future stars settled near the veteran of choice forming a commonwealth of small group discussions covering all things basketball. The daily clusters of advanced questioning and answering expands into a must-attend lecture series with NBA players stressing a universal qualifier: the need for a special skill set to survive "The League."

To reach highest, players must master the tricks of the trade that separate the best from the rest, the craftsmanship we used for the on-court schooling of the baby Terps. One such ploy encourages developing a high-arching shot when finishing around the basket, a prerequisite for NBA point guards, like the textbook 1993 floater Simpkins launches over Hoya defender and future NBA player Don Reid to seal the historic victory. The young Terrapins appreciated the apprenticeship and responded like champs, and the scene on each channel looked like the climax of a sentimental movie: wisdom and self-assurance passed down to bloom into gold.

Winning against Georgetown, a top-fifteen team, in their building propels Maryland into the final phase: refinement. Twenty-two years later, on the College Park campus, a P.G. County kid named Romelo "Melo" Trimble leads third-ranked Maryland over Georgetown in a highly anticipated showdown they called "The Rivalry Renewed." And in November of 2016, another P.G. County star, Anthony Cowan, joined Trimble in Maryland's backcourt to thrill a nationwide television audience with a miraculous comeback to take the rematch in DC. Now two title-winning programs share the Beltway, bound to meet again, and basketball is better when they do. It reminds the super-talented kids in the "DMV" that it's good to stay home.

Dave Dickerson and I arrived on the College Park campus in 1985, privileged to play alongside our idol Lenny Bias in his senior season, and our shared hope to form a lasting connection with "The Man" unites us forever. Traveling beyond the loss of a guiding light is our bond and learning Maryland hired Dave in 1996 to display his distinctive Terrapin shell as an assistant coach lifted a weighted spirit. I asked Coach Williams to consider bringing Dave home, and when we found out that his interview was scheduled for June 19, exactly ten years after we lost "The Man," the irony and symmetry reminded us that everything comes back to Lenny.

The critical decision-makers at Maryland refused to consider a connection to Lenny as an end-all deterrent. Choosing Dave signals that the University is healing. Coach Williams understands what Terrapins are made of and counted Dickerson's capacity to endure as a plus. Valuing his knowledge of the game, the integrity he demonstrated as a rising assistant coach, and the passion Dave felt for his alma mater sealed the deal.

Being at the airport to greet Dave and see the first smile from the new Terrapin coach gives me a memory to reach for when the pain of losing Lenny hits. Dave is living proof you can go home

again and take part in creating a new memory. Traveling down the Baltimore-Washington Parkway is like moving back in time and stirs Dave to recall the fantastic first moments inside Cole Field House as we took our place as scholarship basketball players for the University of Maryland. Turning down the homestretch on Greenbelt Road, with the campus in sight, jars fond memories of living in the locker room and a return to the unanswerable question: how did four of us fit inside the tiny apartments we called the "Knox Boxes?"

A decade beyond having our piece of teenage heaven melt into an American nightmare, we used the skills of self-protection developed while being dragged through hell and shifted our focus to the present and the current state of Maryland Basketball. Thinking of our college days inevitably leads to Lenny, and the deep hurt from losing such a friend triggers a defense mechanism that directs the conversation elsewhere.

News of Walt and Mustaf joining me as tenured summer school instructors at "North Gym" induces a prideful expression of delight from Dave and the instinctive request for a full progress report on the baby Terps. We shuffled Coach Williams stories with NBA chatter while circling "The Quad," parked in the familiar lot behind Cole Field House, and exhaled. We were home. We laughed about piling into the "limo" with Lenny on our way to American University. The brief silence that followed opened the door for the pain to interject, but we gave each other a smile with a brotherly handshake and let the good times shine through.

Walking up to Cole to start a new leg of the journey, I can see Lenny Bias bursting through the tunnel doors ready to conquer the basketball world. Watching Dave walk through the same doors as excited as he was in the first two weeks of June 1986 is the personification of progress. He's a decade of determination stronger, coming home to lead the next generation of Terps by example, and to teach them the hard lessons learned as a disciple of "The Man from Landover."

"Double D" was a rock in the torrential storm that hit us when we were student-athletes in College Park. Dave created success along the path and answered the call from his alma mater to

share a compelling Bias. Coach Dickerson surfaces on the other side a champion, as does the University of Maryland, to a certain extent, secretly resurrected.

Maryland returning to form as a winning basketball program and an NCAA Tournament team symbolizes survival, a debt paid, and sins forgiven. Late in June, ten soul-shaping years after the cruelest moment, confirmation circulates throughout "North Gym" that Coach Williams is reaching back into Maryland's past for the ideal assistant coach to complete a championship drive. Coach Williams chose Dave Dickerson because even today, he is driven by the spirit of a Terrapin.

"Double D" captained our 1988-1989 Terrapin team in every sense and shared a suite with me in Washington Hall, the same suite where Len died only two summers before. Some nights we talked until the early morning but rarely of basketball. In fact, Dave talked and I listened, eager, respectful, and in awe of his example of how courage triumphs over tragedy. "Double D" offered lessons with maturity and meaning behind each word. I credited the fortification of his character to having lived within a nightmare.

Dickerson, Greg Nared, Mitch Kasoff, and Massenburg protected and guided me through a trying first year of college, serving as nurturing teammates and bonded brothers, role models on the journey toward representing a Maryland on the mend. Coach Williams opting for Dave Dickerson brings home a University of Maryland ambassador with a strong moral fiber, the smarts to be a perfect bridge between head coach and the players, and a tremendous belief in resurrection. "Double D" understands the exclusivity of college life as a Maryland basketball player like no other candidate. Surviving the catastrophe on campus in 1986 to succeed beyond imagination leaves Dave highly qualified and coming back to a place dear to the heart: a championship combination. Coach Dickerson encourages winning, in life, through basketball and the lessons from Len Bias. Reaching back for him proves an effective step forward for my Maryland in search of excellence.

That's Terrapin Pride.

CHAPTER 10

NATIONAL **CHAMPIONS**

"Tony, you guys helped us do this. Guys like you and Walt coming back and working with the players made a difference; it helped us win this championship."

—HALL OF FAME COACH GARY WILLIAMS, APRIL 1, 2002

WALT

Other than on the court, in the heat of an iron-willed moment, the best trash-talking happens in NBA locker rooms, and with Maryland atop the NCAA, the Terrapin roars furiously throughout "The League." Steve Francis, the rookie sensation from Maryland, joins Massenburg and me as a Houston Rocket during the 1999-2000 NBA season and at least one of us sported something that shouted "Maryland!" every day. Youthful exuberance urges Steve to lead the Terrapin bandwagon from the opening of training camp, popping into the locker room reciting pre-season polls to start the banter. By rule, the team tolerated the tease and nearly everyone encouraged "Stevie Franchise" to needle Hall of Fame big wheels Hakeem Olajuwon and Charles Barkley into the college hoops conversation, hoping for a classic chuckle from "The Dream" and a side-splitting comment about the "Murlind Turtles" from "Sir Charles." The wave of accomplishment washing over College Park gives free reign to a three-man commando squad determined to dominate locker room bragging rights.

We were the Houston Terps: broadcasting Maryland pride NBA-wide.

Away from the NBA, we discussed the state of Maryland Basketball in a serious mode and our conversations leaned toward those formative summer pickup games gauging status, progress, and individual improvement. During gatherings to watch Terp games, we rotated opinions on the origin of specific moves players executed, marveling at their development, taking credit, deserving or not, for contributing to the evolution. Taking part in the maturation of Obinna Ekezie from the apprentice to "The League" and testing the limitless possibilities of prospects Steve Blake and Chris Wilcox strengthens the fraternal shell. With just cause, we publicized Maryland supremacy from our first team meeting in Houston to well after the final buzzer of the NBA season, and with equal ambition we honored our duty to return to College Park each summer to further a labor of love, the long-standing Terrapin tradition of mentoring.

On the 2001 drive to the first Final Four appearance in the history of Maryland Basketball, the departure of Massenburg from Houston to the Vancouver Grizzlies created a temporary void within "Terrapins West." Steve and I added more bass to our tune to maintain dominion in the trash-talk sessions, and the draft-day acquisition of top-Terp Terence Morris resulted in a three-headed Terrapin reigning in Houston once more. During games, we spoke "Terpology," relating everything to Maryland excellence. Given the sparse number of Blue Devils making noise in "The League" regarding their grand theft of the 2001 title, we basked in the glory of Maryland's top-five ranking, professionally advertising each Terrapin victory along the road to the 2002 championship.

Our allegiance grows stronger as we drive the "My school is better than yours" train across the NBA for three straight years, ruling the morning shoot-around, bus rides, and hotel lounges. Any conversation had the potential to develop into a Maryland story. Nearly all NBA players love representing the high school or college that created them, through good and bad times. Having three Terps on the same NBA team when our alma mater experiences the "One Shining Moment" is an extraordinary occasion. It needed to be celebrated, so we let "The League" know in every way imaginable. We badgered all non-Terrapins until the final day when we emptied our Rocket lockers and headed back to College Park, going home to improve for the next NBA season and aid the baby Terps in defense of the title.

Maryland growing into a championship basketball program after the turmoil we endured should be a lesson to anyone in need of a paradigm of perseverance. It's a gratifying and fantastic cause for the way things transpired. Our determination to emerge from the outer darkness after losing the light was what made everything possible, and the moment my marvelous broadcast partner and Hall of Fame "Voice of the Terps" Johnny Holliday announces, "The Kids have done it," the journey to be the best is complete. The Maryland basketball program, once gloomy and devastated, at last shines brightest.

We win.

Profoundly appreciative, the "Houston Terps" delivered the signature message across the nation and to the world through NBA channels: "Fear the Turtle."

TONY

The NBA takes a break and the stage belongs to the NCAA for Championship Monday as Maryland squares off against Indiana for the 2002 national title. I'm playing for the Memphis Grizzlies but I have the night off. Eighty-two regular season games, constant travel, practice, and league obligations leave little time to schedule personal events during the NBA calendar year. Fortunately, on the grandest evening for Terrapin Basketball, I am commitment-free and only a one-hour flight from Atlanta where the Final Four will do battle.

Without a doubt, Maryland will win.

I call Coach Dickerson from the airport to check the pulse and relay well-wishes from "The Wizard" and Steve Francis. Dave sounds confident and completely at ease. We talk about the culmination: game number 2002 in the storied history of Maryland Basketball, a throwback challenge versus the five-time champion Hoosiers to claim the 2002 NCAA title on April Fool's Day. It just has to be destiny. A Maryland victory will be the reward for trusting the Terrapin Way to Survive and the Georgia Dome the place where a cruel past washes away in the glory of a coronation.

The walk down the stairs to join Dave on the floor for the championship celebration feels like my first day as a freshman on campus, one of the best days of my life, strutting down the steps of Cole Field House to meet "Double D" and start the great Terrapin adventure. Just before the victory hug with Dave, the NCAA Champion coach, I pictured Lenny with us, laughing, closing in to place his arms across our shoulders and pull us together.

We hear him.

We feel him.

Lenny connects us. He brought us to College Park and whenever I see Dave or our teammates, I feel Lenny's long arms around us. The mid-court embrace lasts forever and I think about how far we've come and how much stronger we are compared to the struggle to hold each other up on the morning of June 19, 1986. We are still standing. With the broadest smile I've ever seen on his face, Dave utters the three timeless words every teammate longs to hear: "We did it."

Two more hugs and a handshake of brotherhood later, we separated to spread the love, understanding above all how Terrapins build triumph from tragedy. We grow from a compelling environment.

Watching the television with an eye on Coach Williams and the other one looking for Dave Dickerson makes it hard to dial Massenburg's number. Three rings into the call, Tony answers.

He's in the middle of the festivities, catching confetti with "Double D," and I'm somewhere between laughing and crying. Satisfied. Of the many noble reasons Maryland deserves being on top, be it the University's relentless nature or Coach Williams' ability to build an elite program and an ultra-talented team, "Double D" stands on top. Consider the gamut of emotions Dickerson endured in this triumphant second-chance run through the Final Four with a resuscitated alma mater. He loses a friend and teammate, loses innocence, loses games, and still finds the power to stand tall, to lead us, to create success as a coach, and return home to win the national championship.

Dave is Maryland.

In the gut-wrenching moments after the tough losses, sprawling on locker room floors searching our souls, the weight of the burden carried by my teammates who played with Len Bias may have been too much for me to understand. Nevertheless, Dave and Tony plowed through the most difficult times and grew stronger, refusing to make excuses or allow us baby Terps to believe heartbreak destroys effort. They bravely navigated the Maryland odyssey and reached unimaginable heights to leave an evolving legacy of achievement in College Park and beyond. Their NCAA careers started with a devastating loss but seeing Dickerson and Massenburg sharing the ultimate college victory provides a fitting finale.

Maryland earned the stately position atop the college basketball world, where we belong, and Dave and Tony closed the chapter, together.

Before our commemorative conversation slipped into pure sap, I expressed my gratitude to Massenburg for his contribution, personally and professionally, and asked him to relay the same message to Dave.

After a long pause, Tony sighed and said, "Walt, Lenny can rest."

I thanked God, and the golden silence made it okay to let a tear fall.

I wondered about Coaches Wade and Driesell, and how the big win affects the legends like "Buck" Williams and Albert King. I remembered the talks with Coach Williams about believing you can win every game, backing down from no one, and toughness being contagious. He put us back on the road and had the answer at every turn, even when we couldn't see where we were going.

After a bitter road loss to Duke during my senior season, Coach Williams sat down at my locker for a post-game chat that makes more sense to me with every year that passes. With the pain of the loss written across his face, Coach Williams stressed the significance of fighting to the wire with the number one team in the country, and the impact of our competitiveness on the Maryland fan base and the future of the University.

Back then, I couldn't see it. It was six years to the day that Len Bias carried the Terps over the top-ranked Tar Heels and gave Terrapin fans a victory for the ages, thrusting Maryland Basketball into the national conversation. All I could think of was that by losing to the wicked Blue

Devils, I had fallen short. Coach reinforced his message by planting a seed of hope. He predicted an upset of North Carolina at Cole Field House the next week. The win, Coach said, will put us on the path to a national championship.

Coach walked away and left me staring at the locker in wonder. Despite suffering more losses than Terrapins care to remember, our coach believed in us making a run for the 1992 title. I stood up to second the notion.

No doubt, Coach.

We can.

We are Maryland, every bit as good as Duke and North Carolina.

A decade passes before I realize the intent of his 1992 talk about winning it all. The national championship drives home the point. Coach Williams described a vision of Maryland Basketball growing elite by building on competitiveness. He looked beyond who we were at that moment to see what we would become. Ten years later, on April Fool's Day, 2002, Coach seems remarkably prophetic. We win. And yes, we did deliver the upset victory against the tenth-ranked Tar Heels in 1992, just as Coach called it. We were on the path.

After Coach Williams cuts down the definitive victory net and swirls the keepsake toward heaven for all to see, Dickerson leads the way through the maze to greet and applaud our chief for completing the mission. Coach Williams turns to see the two of us beaming, clenches his jaws, shakes my hand, and declares, "Tony, you guys helped us do this. Guys like you and Walt coming back and working with the players made a difference. It helped us win this championship."

I saluted Coach for closing the chapter and with a second handshake of solidification we separated, forever connected. Dave drifted toward the players. I stayed near the basket to capture every angle of happiness, and when Coach Williams raises

his fist toward the Terrapin faithful in the stands, my alumni pride turns the clock back.

Sharing the 2002 NCAA championship celebration with Dave Dickerson and Coach Williams on the floor of the Georgia Dome is the culmination of a journey that originated in despair. The victory signals that Maryland is on a new road, a paved highway, and the Terrapin family is leaving the mud and dust of the past behind.

Coaches Williams, Dickerson, and Jimmy Patsos insist that I join the team in the locker room and fully participate in the championship experience. I celebrated as if I had suited up and played, thrilled, knowing I had done my best to teach these players everything Lenny and the NBA taught me. That's the brotherhood at Maryland.

Coach Williams summarizes the journey for the freshly crowned squad by recalling something he claims he often shares with his players. He tells them how, less than a week after I completed my first year in the NBA, I was back in Cole Field House, improving my game, and spreading the knowledge. Coach talked about me working in the gym five and six times a week, lifting, playing, and talking with the team, and points to that work ethic and commitment as the essential values that are the foundation of the Maryland program. He thanked me again for contributing to the championship evolution and his words, together with the love from the team, allows this old Terp to sip from the victory cup.

I let Coach Williams and the players know that I only did what needed to be done, as the top Terps did for me. Schooling the youngsters grew into a rite of passage for Terrapin basketball players. I cherished the responsibility of serving as the next Maryland Professor of Pickup with an NBA degree.

I prospered from working with, playing against, and studying Lenny Bias, learning the keys to maximize my skills. Jerrod Mustaf and I circled back home to indoctrinate "The Wizard" and Evers Burns. They earned NBA degrees and rebounded to campus to carry on the tradition, building the competitiveness necessary for a first-class program. Partnering with Walt and a procession of

Maryland aces coming home for the summer to move beyond the opposition, a passion drenches Terrapin basketball and infuses a secret ingredient into the resurrection.

After the championship whirlwind in the Georgia Dome, Coach Dickerson and I reunited at his hotel to apply the finishing touch to an extra-special day. We sparked celebratory cigars while gazing over the Atlanta cityscape, contemplating the magnitude of the moment, reminiscing. Every story that evokes the memory of Lenny Bias and his untimely death now ends on an uplifting note.

We did it.

And to all those who said Maryland would never recover: late in the evening on April 1, 2002, we won game number 2002, and came out on top.

No fooling.

I hustled back to Memphis for our morning practice session wearing an oversized jacket, looking for one person, one particular teammate. Zipping past head coach Sidney Lowe, a DC native, ACC legend, and NCAA champion, and neglecting our normal greeting nearly exposes my plan.

With perfect timing, the coat slides off my shoulders and reveals a fresh Maryland 2002 National Champions shirt so that Shane Battier could take a good long look. Yes, that man, the Blue Devil himself, who stole the 2001 title from us long before helping LeBron James and the Miami Heat win consecutive NBA championships. Surely burning inside, Battier respectfully bows his head, recognizing that this moment belongs to Maryland, and I know he fears the Terrapin like the rest of the college basketball world, and all is well.

The Joe Smith squads and the 2002 national championship team present a striking similarity: Smith and Juan Dixon put on phenomenal performances, Exree Hipp and Chris Wilcox demonstrated freakish athleticism, Johnny Rhodes and Byron Mouton delivered heart and soul,

Duane Simpkins and Steve Blake provided solid and steady extensions of Coach Williams, while Keith Booth and Lonny Baxter applied brute force. The bricks of the road: cut from the same stone.

During my career in College Park, our state of affairs hampered national recruiting. Appealing to the regional high school standout and his affinity for our locale may have been the only option and our 1990s fabulous five came through for Terrapin fans in spectacular fashion. In 2002, only starters Dixon and Baxter entered College Park from the "DMV." Blake, Mouton, and Wilcox along with fellow champions Tahj Holden, Drew Nicholas and Ryan "Sleepy" Randle ranked among the best from outside our area, collectively attracted to what we established at Maryland by overcoming the stigma and becoming "The U.C.L.A. of the East" that former Terp Jay McMillen and Coach Driesell envisioned.

The on-court success of the 1992 and 1993 classes of recruits enabled the Maryland basketball staff to venture beyond the "DMV" and draw from an increasingly expansive pool of talent. College Park catches not just the interest of Laron Profit from nearby Delaware and Terrell Stokes from the famed Simon Gratz of Pennsylvania but crosses the oceans to lure Lithuanian Sarunas Jasikevicius and Obinna Ekezie from Nigeria, and the player who shares the single-game assist title with Terrell Stokes, the great Greivis Vasquez of Venezuela.

The doors are officially open for the return to recruiting as usual. The ascent back to where we belong, achieved with such great effort, makes Terrapin coaches welcome in the homes of the best young basketball players where they can compete with the best for their commitment. As a consequence, Marylanders Terence Morris and Steve Francis turn up on the national stage while shining inside the hometown arena, in front of family and friends on the "Field House" court, the location of their childhood dreams. And, a kid named Juan Dixon realizes his purpose, dazzling the college basketball world by playing for the team he "...grew up loving while watching my favorite player, 'The Wizard,' on the local Baltimore channels."

The rest is NCAA championship history.

Chapter 11

LIFE AFTER "THE LEAGUE"

"When a dream ends, when a shooting star leaves us breathless, we see the beauty in our time together."

WALT

I retired from the NBA in 2003 after we lost to the San Antonio Spurs in the Western Conference Finals, my second trip to the Conference Finals and the second time the Spurs dashed my championship hopes. In 1999, as a member of the Portland Trailblazers, San Antonio great Sean Elliot sank us with a game-winning three-pointer the pundits call "the Memorial Day Miracle." The Spurs make waves every year and when Tony called to say San Antonio offered him a contract for the 2005 season, I saw the black and silver championship banner, and I responded with wholehearted congratulations as the Terrapin inside me thought, "Finally, Massenburg will collect the prize he, more than anyone in the NBA, deserves."

The time a teenager spends in college can be the greatest and most exciting period of his or her life and being a scholarship student-athlete should enhance that experience. The brotherhood forged on the court, inside the locker room, and during the heat of battle often becomes a bond stronger than friends, even stronger than family.

I cannot imagine life after losing a teammate during my career at Maryland. Tony Massenburg simply would not accept defeat and pressed relentlessly forward amid constant turmoil. He never gave in to circumstances.

It was a righteous moment when "Big Young'un" won, and stood on the world championship platform receiving his just reward.

A great guy finished first.

TONY

San Antonio bookends my NBA storyline by drafting me, setting me on a fantastic voyage from Barcelona, Spain to Vancouver, Canada, and bringing me back to south-central Texas for a first-place finish.

A mid-summer call to rejoin San Antonio for a run at the 2005 crown paralyzes me—that's what happens to free agents when the Spurs show interest—I looked at the telephone and saw a career-defining championship ring on my finger. Full of momentum from first prize finishes in 1999 and 2003, the Spurs in the pre-season looked like a shoo-in to reach the final round in 2005, and my spine still tingles as I recall the moment when the unlikely and enviable opportunity to play on a team chasing an NBA title crosses from dream into reality.

Before the ink dries on the contract, a second vision strikes. Coming into "The League" with San Antonio in 1990, I looked forward to wearing number thirty-four, of course, but the great Terry Cummings staked a veteran's claim to the thirty-four Spurs jersey and wore it well. The night the 2005 Spurs expressed interest in signing me, I searched online for their 2004 team photograph and made a wonderful discovery: jersey number thirty-four is available for the 2005 season.

During the double-check of the San Antonio roster, a vivid image of Lenny Bias with the golden NBA championship trophy protrudes from the computer screen the way a stereogram shocks the mind. His comforting smile broadens my smile; the thirty-four jersey ripples in three dimensions, and the magic visual melts into perpetual inspiration. Eight weeks later, a Spurs practice uniform

hangs inside a locker with "MASSENBURG" in big letters across the back above a bold number thirty-four and, every day going forward toward the NBA title, the shrine-like presence of a glistening thirty-four jersey reminds me that Lenny will be a champion forever.

On the way to a fourth NBA World Championship, Tim Duncan suffers an ankle sprain and misses twelve of the final sixteen regular season games. I'm tapped to play at a Hall of Fame level during the spring rush for home-court advantage and the Spurs' championship aspirations. At thirty-seven-years old, playing meaningful minutes in a playoff push, having teammates count me a contributing member of a world-class organization—at last everything basketball falls into place.

Retirement takes a back seat to rejuvenation.

Duncan recovers and is strong as ever for the stretch run to secure home-court advantage in the Western Conference. Winning the right to host the decisive seventh game of The Finals gives us the edge to dethrone the Detroit Pistons and the postgame focus on family and togetherness leaves me leaning toward another run. Fifteen years of service and the invigorating pursuit of the elusive championship doubles my appetite for the exuberance NBA basketball offers, the delectable, intangible passion fruit.

The sight of the gleaming gold Larry O'Brien trophy rolling toward the stage sends a charge through a rapturous SBC Center and a sense of accomplishment across the podium of distinction. The loudspeakers blast Freddie Mercury and Queen singing "We are the Champions." NBA Commissioner David Stern crowns Tim Duncan a three-time Finals MVP and the wholesome bliss of a third-grade award banquet fills a thirsty soul. During the transition for team photographs, I ask six-time champion Robert Horry to describe his feelings after winning more rings than fingers on a hand. Horry, known throughout the world as "Big Shot Rob," shouts, "The next one is always sweeter," and it echoes in the ears of each player on the stage. The all-in mentality necessary to win the 2005 Championship ignites a rally cry to expand the San

Antonio dynasty and become modern-day reminders to "Remember the Alamo."

A blessing allows my parents and son T.J. to stand beside me as World Championship ticker tape rains from the rafters. In anticipation of raising the golden NBA trophy, I feel this triumphant occasion as if it was shining a light on my long journey. Between the hugs and the high fives, I fought a surge of tears as each disaster I had to overcome to reach this life-changing accomplishment appears extraordinarily brilliant in my mind's eye. Many within the Spurs organization understood the complexity of my travels and travails, and their personal expressions of pure joy that I had won a championship after laboring through unparalleled adversity reaches deep into my heart.

Gazing through confetti, absorbing the resonance of approval from the crowd, I thought of my classmates from Maryland. I thought of the friend we lost that terrible day in June. I wanted him there to tell him "thank you" for accepting me, shielding me, and setting me on this path. I stood on top of the basketball world, a teammate of Lenny Bias, and from the pinnacle, I see "The Man" smile, feel his arm across my shoulders again, and hear his voice once more say, "Yea, Big Young'un."

During the locker room celebration of the 2005 NBA championship, I stepped away from the limelight for a moment to pinch myself and preserve the champagne-soaked, number thirty-four Spurs jersey. Without warning, future first ballot Hall of Fame inductee Tim Duncan creeps up from behind and calmly douses me with a fresh bottle, saying, "Congratulations, champ. You deserve this. We did it for you, ACC baby."

After delivering the champagne shower, Duncan skips away, possibly recognizing Maryland on my mind, fully aware of the Lenny Bias factor, and our heartrending struggle to survive losing "The Man." Staring at the number thirty-four on that championship jersey, holding the premium basketball prize, my only desire is a longing to be back in Leonardtown Hall, playing card games, and shooting the breeze with my Terrapin teammates. A lump develops in my throat as I imagine my brothers watching me on the podium, raising a collective glass to share the incredible sensation.

We won. We all won.

The University of Maryland family and the world of Terrapin fans with an appreciation for the journey beyond a shooting star won as well, because College Park shaped one more champion.

Number thirty-four.

Spending time with T.J. in Texas and training with the Spurs allowed the San Antonio front office and their version of the "Big Three:" Duncan, Emanuel "Manu" Ginóbili, and William "Tony" Parker, to develop a flattering appreciation of my dedication and professionalism. Learning that Tim Duncan, one of the most respected athletes in America, recommended me to his Spurs organization as an asset for the 2005 unit confirms the achievement of a principal ambition in team sports: Peer Acknowledgement.

The magical moments of elation following the classic game-seven victory over the defending champion Detroit Pistons have only one rival: befriending my sports hero and being welcomed into his Terrapin family during my official visit to the University of Maryland. The idyllic celebrations precisely represent my full-circle NBA expedition. San Antonio three-time NBA Coach of the Year Gregg Popovich, the longest-tenured NBA head coach and a surefire Hall of Fame candidate, served as an assistant with the Spurs during my first year in "The League." The leader of our 1990-1991 Spurs team, Hall of Fame coach Larry Brown, happened to be calling the shots on the opposing sideline as we battled his Pistons during the 2005 NBA Finals.

Coach Brown had given me the rookie Spur treatment; discipline and desire occasionally butted heads but his wisdom and direction proved on point. At the conclusion of the championship series, with the two teams exchanging congratulations and well-wishing, I searched for Coach Brown to let him know I listened and followed his counsel. Coach Brown tugs on me first. I turned to extend my hand, eager to voice gratitude for being drafted and for the early, critical guidance. Side-stepping the handshake, Coach Brown delivers a grizzly bear hug with an unforgettable sentiment: "No one deserves this more than you." The memory of this magnificent moment with Coach Brown causes time to stand still in admiration of an emotional high point along the demanding journey, and the circle turns gold.

The world championship glow inside the packed SBC Center sparks my imagination with visions of Lenny and his family commemorating NBA championship celebrations in Boston, base-building opportunities for Maryland fans to celebrate Terrapin pride. Losing Lenny changed the direction of life, and my anonymous journey through "The League" beyond that cruel moment leaves the worldwide audience unfamiliar with the guy wearing the number thirty-four jersey for the 2005 NBA champs. A few times each NBA season, someone mentioned me teaming with Lenny Bias, immediately and often notoriously warping my identity. My Terrapin family and fans experiencing a similar sting from an affiliation with Lenny may have enjoyed a special celebration the night we captured the NBA championship and may take solace going forward.

Every College Park student, fan, administrator, and educator contributed to the resurrection of our program and thereafter, when a Maryland guy wins a world championship, Terrapins everywhere win. The struggle against depression significantly influenced the shaping of our enduring, fearsome character, a favorable feature emerging from dreadful trials and tribulations. We are products of our experiences, grand and terrible.

We win.

Wearing Lenny's number during my final season as a basketball player honors my friend and, being immortalized, seizing and kissing the golden trophy with jersey number thirty-four as the backdrop will stand as a testament to our saga. The record books prove a Maryland Terrapin wins an NBA world championship in 2005. A thorough inspection of the San Antonio championship roster will reveal a former Terp wearing the number thirty-four. With optimism, the sharp focus will lead to a reflection on the lessons from Lenny as well.

After my NBA run in 2003 with the Dallas Mavericks, I was satisfied with giving eleven years to "The League," and it was time for my family. Midway through the summer of 2003, a telephone call puts my resolve to the test.

Danny Ainge, President of Basketball Operations for the Boston Celtics, calls to express interest in my services, saying that, along with future Hall of Fame star Paul Pierce, I could play an important role in their vision for Beantown. I listened to this enticing proposition while refereeing a game being played by a league of ten-year-olds. The five-second countdown grabs my attention and a youngster nicknamed "Old School" drops in a three-pointer at the buzzer to end the morning session on a high note and send the camp to lunch. The kids mobbed "Old School" at half-court, the camp counselors smacked high-fives and chest-bumps, and the families on the sidelines erupted, amazed and elated.

I sank into the bleachers, whistle in mouth, purely happy. I pressed the button to replay the voice message and passed the telephone to a good buddy to hear the siren call from Boston. His joyful expression dims down to a dubious stare. He tosses the telephone back to me and, with a hint of perplexity, replies, "You and number thirty-four."

He then darts off to rejoin the buzzer-beating party leaving me staring, remembering Paul Pierce wearing number thirty-four for the Boston Celtics. I'm thinking about Bias and the Celtics, Paul Pierce and the possibility of postponing retirement, and my head gets heavy and shakes in denial. The encore celebration of happy campers singing and dancing with "Old School" on the shoulders of both coaches, getting the hero's ride to the lunchroom, a family-focused roof-raising, shows me that life after the NBA will be just fine.

Time to blow the whistle.

Someone mentions that surviving the difficult years in College Park bridged the gap and laid the foundation for Maryland Basketball to become a championship program and the sense of accomplishment feels better than all of my on-court victories combined. A goal born from the negativity surrounding Terrapin Basketball, the University of Maryland, Prince George's County, and Len Bias—everything I love—expands into a plan for life, a plan to bring good tidings to College Park, and help Maryland grow into a perennial national contender. Today, the little light shining on the concrete connection between the Bias-driven desire to play for Maryland, staying Terrapin true, and winning the championship seems like divine vindication.

Good people questioned my decision to turn down Dean Smith and the top-tier Tar Heels for a College Park in recovery. Some frowned on my staying in school and delaying the NBA–twice.

In my heart, I know they were good decisions: being the seventh pick in the draft and a college graduate helps quiet the critics. Maryland going to eleven straight NCAA tournaments, consecutive Final Fours, and bringing home the national championship tells the world that our university profited from the lessons as well.

The Terrapin: Deliberate and Steady.

Less than two months after winning the 2005 NBA Finals, an ugly ankle fracture crushes any idea of a repeat run with the Spurs but, as the Bias blueprint stipulates, two decades of grief-driven perseverance kicks in and I go back to work.

A two-year stretch of intense physical therapy adds a new dimension of endurance and flexibility, the nagging injuries from twenty years of hard knocks fall away a bit, the hunger for NBA basketball never stops burning, and in the fall of 2007, I'm invited to join the Washington Wizards training camp squad, with a shared belief that a new generation of athletes will benefit from the lessons I learned in my journey. Time lost to rehabilitation and salary cap restrictions hampered negotiations, but staging a fulfilling return to taste one last sip of life in "The League" soothes my soul. I had offers from several attractive suitors but in the final appraisal, finishing where I started, and going out on top with the champion Spurs is the clear answer.

Alpha to Omega.

The spirit of Lenny Bias lives within me, and much of who I am results from his life. During the joyful moments, I see Lenny's smile and the smiles on the faces of his family and friends greeting him after a game. I think of the teenaged fans at today's Terrapin

games sporting the number thirty-four Maryland jersey because an old Terp told them his story, and they love him. In hard times, memories of cross-campus walks with "The Man," talking about the love we have for our parents—lionhearted fathers and amazing mothers—and the need to make a path for those young ones in doubt gives me courage to go on.

Because I can.

The many successes I experienced as a basketball player and the fortitude to reach beyond the challenges of life are results of having been a Maryland Terrapin during those infamous dark days in College Park. Lenny Bias set the stage and surviving the aftermath of his passing tested my determination, making me strong. Without the painful moments in my past, I would be a vastly different man.

As it stands, I am a World Champion, living beyond expectation.

"The Man from Landover" leaves a most important legacy: Be great and beware.

Thank you, Lenny. We forward the lesson.

Personal and institutional success vanishes in light of losing Len too young. Focusing on the circumstances surrounding the cruel moment stirs empathy, anguish and anger, so we find peace and resolution accentuating the inspirational twenty-two years of life. The Len Bias legacy sets in motion a series of events that pave the way for Maryland to earn the first NCAA basketball championship in school history, a position in the top tier of public research schools, and a top-50 ranking among world universities.

We rise.

When a community experiences a tragedy, each person dedicated to the region carries it in his or her heart. Sports fans from the "DMV" bear a permanent scar from losing Len Bias, and the diverse measures of pain and redemption always affect us, but using grief as a driver to get the most out of life is an admirable alternative.

"Post-Bias" basketball players with ties to the Washington, DC area inherited a chip on their shoulders capable of creating a unique drive, and overachieving becomes impossible when greatness is the goal.

I walked a fine line to crush the scarlet letter on Prince George's County basketball players. We fed on community pride to represent Maryland despite a national outpouring of venom, and our ardent supporters cheered for their Terps because the loyal never abandon ship. Each player who wore the Terrapin uniform, every administrator who steered us through the cloud, the coaches who committed themselves to fostering our development, and every fan who refused to let strife quiet Cole Field House earned the joy accompanying the championship celebration because we all share the pain of losing Len Bias.

Many Marylanders—from devoted Terrapin followers to those who know little of college basketball—shed tears at our heartbreak. With the Terps standing atop the college basketball world, fans everywhere recognized that Maryland was finally getting its due, rewarded with the moment in time we dearly deserved, for our era of suffering, and for staying true.

Sweet.

The lessons from Lenny started to unfold when he tipped the college basketball world by knocking down a game-winning shot against the University of Tennessee at Chattanooga in the first round of the 1983 NCAA Tournament. Growing up in Virginia between Maryland and Tobacco Road, that decisive jumper registered a resounding victory for my Atlantic Coast Conference and another big-time basket from an ACC freshman.

I liked Len Bias. He appeared to be easy to like. The pretty jump shot, muscle and grace meshed to perfection, commanded widespread admiration. He was my kind of ballplayer. I followed his progress the next season and the MVP performance that led the Terrapins to the 1984 ACC Tournament championship fortified my Lenny "bias."

"The Man from Landover" created the most significant change that can happen to any teenager: Lenny inspired in me the need to achieve. I tracked the connection between Bias and the ball on both ends of the court during his televised games and highlights; I listened to each word of his interviews, and I impersonated number thirty-four from Maryland as preparation for my scholarship auditions. As I laced up my shoes to play, I became Bias. I hit the Virginia courts on a mission to be a force, like "The Man."

Len's basketball wizardry was brilliant athleticism on any court. "The Man from Landover" selected Cole Field House, removed the Georgetown jacket from my back, and replaced it with a Diamondback shell. He enhanced my sense of pride in being a Marylander once restrained by regional "Hoya-mania." My birth certificate gives me the right to claim "The District" but my loyalty resides in my house and with my P.G. County community, with Len Bias drawing me across the line.

Len decided to stay, play, and excel at home and that delivered an impressive message: Supporting Georgetown is territorially no different than rooting for Howard University or American University. We were winning in College Park, in Prince George's County, and Marylanders who loved basketball began to see the Terrapins as "their home team." Len Bias made the Turtle cool, a perceptibly monumental task in the Washington, DC region of that time.

Yes, many fans ran away from post-Bias Maryland but that, too, was a challenge that drew me toward College Park, determined to find and redefine success.

The Len Bias legacy reinforces three critical inspirational values for victory against any situation:

- I can fight to win every day, come what may
- a triumphant outcome is possible
- even under the worst conditions, a person can rise, and steer the course of their life.

Len's death and the national spotlight that uncovered questions concerning the academic performance of student-athletes in College Park created a negative caricature of a Maryland basketball player. This unfair criticism amplified my need to dispel the notion of P.G. County and Maryland athletes not succeeding as both scholars and sportsmen. The same way Len Bias demonstrated his remarkable ability to achieve, I wanted to earn a degree while ripping through the ACC to prove that our community can produce elite student-athletes. The revelation of academic shortcomings simply clarified the way forward and was another incentive to steer my efforts.

We grow from "The Man."

The offer from Coach Driesell to join Lenny Bias rewarded and strengthened the character I inherited from my parents and supported their life-long examples of hard work, sacrifice, and dedication. I lived a dream playing basketball with my idol for a year, and without notice, the dream eroded as Lenny passed on his greatest lesson: Mortality. At eighteen years old, I lost a friend and it destroyed my idea of a wonderful world. Being plunged into a cruel existence darkens everything.

But over time, a new man takes shape, evolves, and rises again.

Len Bias left one option for me. I needed to do well, and play well because I couldn't see that my world could survive with anything less than my absolute best. During the darkest time, we lived on the brink, aching for success. Difficult circumstances dominated College Park when I selected the University of Maryland, but I trusted my teammates' desire and ability to strive for greatness, as individuals and as a team, and to rise again.

Leaving the Terrapins behind when life demanded time to recuperate would have contradicted my duty to deliver a first-class performance at Maryland. Achieving may allow me to speak highly of Len and give the sports world opportunities to say good things when talking about Maryland.

Ultimately, we received a righteous reward. The Maryland basketball program survived and thrived, and by honoring my commitment and staying true to the Terps during the sanctions, a booming self-confidence grew in my heart. This was what drove me to succeed in the NBA and, most important, to win at life.

I journey beyond the heartbreak believing I can do this.

I can. Maryland can.

In basketball retirement, I think of Lenny Bias more than ever, even more than when I dreamed of being "The Man." What we survived and what has come to pass influences every aspect of my daily life. Before leaving the house each morning, sometimes before rising from bed, a song or the news or just the silence carries a memory of Lenny and our long, arduous journey. Time presents a true picture of all that Lenny accomplished, wondrous and shocking, and I feel the anxiety of 1986 and the bright lights of the future every day. I focus on the greatness that made Lenny a two-time ACC Player of the Year in order to capitalize on my potential. Losing a devoted son to a cruel moment remains the ultimate lesson.

"The Man" converted Marylanders to Terrapins and rekindled a deep affection. The "Lefty" Driesell teams remain among the most decorated in school history but, during my adolescent years, Terrapin popularity faded in the hearts of the "hoopers" playing at the parks and recreation centers around the "DMV." Georgetown Basketball stomped its way in and became an established dynasty in the capital city. The Hoyas won, with locals filling the roster, and that captured the passions of almost everyone I knew. Len Bias arrived on the scene, led Maryland to an ACC Tournament championship, and demanded our attention.

Because Len blossomed in the arid and stony soil of Prince George's County, we loved him beyond sport. Bias would shine as an amazing college player at any university but opting for the hometown team made Len, "The Man." If Len Bias had sprouted from another part of the country and chosen to play for the University of Maryland, his fabulous performance inevitably would have won a certain devotion and his death would still have been a terrible misfortune.

But Len played high school basketball within walking distance of Cole Field House, exemplified what we believed was best about Prince George's County, and represented everything we hoped for in Maryland.

For that, he became our native son.

I have always been puzzled by the concept that Superman would have a weakness. If I accept that Superman existed, I struggled to grasp how "The Man of Steel" could conquer everything except some green substance with a paralyzing glow. Stopping bullets and trains, leaping skyscrapers, outracing rockets, and holding down an office job were things I wanted to do along with millions of other kids. Seeing kryptonite sapping Superman of his strength brought on my earliest memory of anger.

My father sat down with me and explained that Superman, a comic book creation, needed a weakness to demonstrate that even a Man of Steel must recognize there are things in this world that are stronger, failure is always possible, and heroism must always be earned.

Discovering the secret of Santa Claus caused less disappointment. Creating a superhero with a weakness instead of making him invincible did not make any sense. Today, this childhood puzzle embodies the primary lesson I learned from Lenny. Heroes, real and imagined, have flaws. Likewise, real people, whether a paperboy or the king of the court, can always fall.

During my freshman year at Maryland, Lenny was the Superman of college basketball. The true occupation of the College Park Clark Kent may remain a mystery and unknown to most, but

at the high point of his time among mortals, we realized "The Man" was more human than we ever imagined, with a weakness, a tragic flaw. It took him down but, like Superman, the images, records, and influence of Lenny Bias will live for generations in the hearts of those who know the journey.

My friend. My teammate.

A superhero.

The DC area basketball players of today have parents and guardians who live with the lessons we hope to spread, and because of this, our kids come of age in an environment where they grow to know that succeeding at basketball is expected and, therefore, constructively challenging. We can tell the up and coming ball players that greatness came from our region once and surely can come again.

If a young ball player from the "DMV" wants to become great, their mentors only have to point to number thirty-four to show what the greatest looked like. Len Bias was a regular kid from P.G. County who loved basketball so much that he achieved greatness from simply living out his dream.

One lesson is: he achieved. We can, too.

The other lesson is: he made a terrible, irreparable mistake and the result is engraved in our hearts. The picture of our icon falling to earth lessens the chance that the young will repeat his error. We can follow "The Man" on the court and use the knowledge gained from his shortcomings away from the court to make better decisions.

Watching confetti fall on former Maryland football star Torrey Smith after he helped the Philadelphia Eagles win Super Bowl Fifty-Two touched the Terp in me. I felt the same way in 2016 watching Terrapin Vernon Davis celebrate a championship with Peyton Manning and the Denver Broncos. I remembered Smith

playing for the Baltimore Ravens, outlasting Davis' San Francisco 49ers to win Super Bowl Forty-Seven, and it reminded me that even during the darkest days, College Park was a haven for great student-athletes.

Under Armour™, a Terrapin creation, is now a global brand; more than a few Terps were in the 2016 Olympics; the champion Lady Terrapins have dominated Big Ten basketball; both women's and men's lacrosse teams were National Champions in 2017; the baseball squad reached new heights, and Maryland soccer standouts Graham Zusi and Omar Gonzalez bolstered the United States Men's National Team on the way to the "Knockout Round" of the World Cup in Brazil.

Lenny did not deny them.

My number forty-two jersey soaring above the court next to the untouchable thirty-four once worn by Len Bias symbolizes the passage, the link, an eternal bridge connecting the rough road we crossed with the open road to better days. The warm and rowdy applause from the Cole Field House faithful as the University of Maryland honors my forty-two jersey takes me back to that sixteen-year-old kid again, crying in disbelief as I listen to the news of Len's death. But that moment created change in the dream, a turn toward clear goals: follow Len to College Park, strive to match his unattainable excellence, and give Maryland, my home, reasons to cheer again.

We live with reminders of the loss, as individuals, as a community, a program, and a university, and yet we move beyond the sorrow. Maryland deserves to celebrate, and I remain grateful for the privilege to play a small part in a triumphant recovery of joy.

Nothing takes away the pain in my chest that comes when I think of losing "The Man." It never fades, but a glance into the rafters before the Terps step onto Gary Williams Court gives me an unequaled sense of victory, and without fail, love focuses my eyes on number thirty-four, insisting that I remember that I was so fortunate to have Len Bias to love.

Next in line to Bias, my number forty-two waves with the jerseys of the outstanding players that followed us, adding to the ageless legacy. We form a fascinating combination: The legend, the bridge, and the road to a championship program.

The life of Len Bias resonates throughout the "DMV," and Maryland athletes are privileged to be raised by a generation of leaders who watched, learned from, and lost "The Man." Beltway basketball scores high marks, a product of a distinctive regional passion for excellence. At least eight players on playoff rosters vying for the 2013 NBA championship received basketball schooling in Prince George's County, including Thomas Robinson, Sam Young, Roy Hibbert, Keith Bogans, Jarrett Jack, Tywon Lawson, Jeff Green, and Kevin Durant, with Michael Beasley, Dante Cunningham, Victor Oladipo, Chinanu Onuaku, and brothers Jerian and Jerami Grant joining the distinguished list in the years that followed.

Highlights of Jeff Green excelling as a multidimensional forward with the Boston Celtics gives P.G. County a precious combination of sentiment and accomplishment. Green, born in P.G. County during that terrible summer of 1986, was a star for Northwestern High School, like Bias, and at six-feet-nine, plays with a graceful versatility in the mold of his Wildcat predecessor. His play adds poetry to an extraordinary connection. The Los Angeles Clippers acquired Jeff Green in February of 2016 to shore up a shot at an NBA title. During an Internet search for details on the trade, a photograph pops up showing Jeff in Celtic Green, chest-passing the ball, an ordinary picture until I noticed his teammate, Brandon Bass, wearing number thirty.

The sudden flash of the green number thirty jersey makes me think of another picture taken June 23, 1986 in Cole Field House as Jesse Jackson and "Red" Auerbach present Mrs. Bias the number thirty Celtics jersey her son earned, and it hurts for a while, as it should. But five months later, Jeff Green chooses to wear number thirty-four for the Orlando Magic, and in a blink, I am lifted and leveled by the intersection of thirty years of achievement with the "The Man" and the moment. In the starting lineup for the Boston Celtics in game one of the 2017 Conference Semi-Finals against the Washington Wizards, I see Gerald Green wearing number thirty. A few rows behind the basket, in a sea of green and white, sits a fan wearing a gold Maryland Terrapin jersey with the red thirty-four beaming through my television screen like a neon light: Len Bias.

The journey continues.

I am living testimony to the changes in "DMV" basketball during the latter half of the 1980's, maturing within the aftermath, and it strikes me that I am not alone. Three decades infused with the life and lessons of Len Bias have created one of the most talent-rich basketball regions in the country. The men and women who mentor, coach, and support the young "DMV" athletes of today have the life of Len Bias to guide them and, because of this, I believe that they mentor, coach, and inspire with a singular passion. Perhaps the dark clouds that descended over our region in 1986 created a superior learning environment, and the results are revealed in the rise of our new young stars.

It's no surprise that the first three starters introduced to the global audience tuning in to the 2016 NCAA Championship basketball game grew up in Maryland, and a fourth Marylander came off the bench to lead the champion Villanova Wildcats in scoring. P.G. County's Nate Britt winning the 2017 NCAA title and Markelle Fultz being the first overall pick in the 2017 NBA draft confirms what we already know. They're on a golden path followed by a long line of local stars like Kevin Durant and Tywon Lawson. At almost seven feet tall, Durant, the 2007 College Player of the Year, four-time NBA scoring champion, 2014 NBA MVP and Olympic gold medalist, 2017 and 2018 NBA Champion and Finals MVP from Suitland, Maryland plays with the skill and athleticism of a point guard. Lawson, from Clinton, Maryland, an NCAA champion, 2013 Team USA Basketball camper, and the leader in scoring, assists and steals for the 2014 and 2015 Denver Nuggets, pilots franchises with the streetball determination expected of a six-foot floor general from the "DMV."

Durant and Lawson, kids I remember working out together on the College Park campus, show our youth that sometimes where you come from matters.

Check the rosters.

The "DMV" knows the game.

History stamps "Certified in Basketball" on our calling cards and résumés.

Along with great systems and "X" and "O" schemes, coaches in the

"DMV" lead from the place where pain becomes competitiveness and stubborn determination. Many of the youth league, high school, and Amateur Athletic Union (AAU) coaches from the Washington, DC area have compelling personal memories of journeying beyond the loss of Len Bias. That intimate heartache has a more profound effect on behavior than a cyberspace story or a televised version of the account. For us, Len Bias is always right around the corner.

"The Man" presents a convincing example: Attain a level of excellence admired by all.

Now everyone, pay attention.

Drugs kill!

For some, the death of Len Bias ends the story. For many of the survivors, the lesson unfolds in a different order.

Drugs kill!

Len Bias is the greatest. I can be great, too.

The life of Lenny Bias may have paved a way for subsequent Terps to experience an exceptional stay in College Park. Conceivably, the students at the University of Maryland gained a new awareness and so exist in a safer, more informed environment because Lenny lived, and as they mature, they come to appreciate the full legacy of Lenny Bias. Clarifying his impact is our goal and a primary message in the lessons. Walt and I are optimistic and believe all who value the courage to tackle adversity will consider these lessons from Lenny.

Lenny Bias remains the most significant Terrapin basketball player in the history of the University of Maryland and, as sports journalist and current ESPN co-host Bomani Jones states, without question, "The Man" may be the twentieth century's most influential sports person.

Lenny provides a crash course in Decision-Making 101:

- **How to work**
- **how to maximize talent**

- **how to dominate**
- **how a single bad choice can change everything**

American society, institutions, laws, and sports, my teammates and coaches, the 2002 national championship, the Xfinity Center, and future Terrapins, were all shaped by the impact of "The Man from Landover." Lenny Bias will forever be *that* Terrapin who attracted us, dazzled us, and shocked us to carry on stronger.

We tell the story and frame the legacy.

People who know basketball get the message: When shooting hoops in or around Maryland, be prepared, because winning at basketball means much more than winning a game. We rarely play basketball for fun or exercise. We play basketball to excel.

The best is our standard, the reason why so many NBA players and executives have ties to the Maryland area. P.G. County producing scores of top-notch ball players over the past thirty years is not a coincidence. When a star athlete reaches the top and falls, most of the world focuses on the fall and rightly so. His community remembers the rise, as we should. The fall is sudden and makes a powerful statement. With an unobstructed view, an admiration for the inspiring rise adds life to the lesson.

Len Bias used cocaine. I will not.

Done!

Len Bias steadily improved into one of the greatest college basketball players ever. I will reach my potential by focusing on being great.

I see the silver lining in the cloud through which some view the life of Lenny Bias. People mark the death of our All-American as instrumental in their decision to abstain from cocaine and drugs. His tragic mistake is still the ultimate anti-drug message.

Lenny may have affected drug use and litigation to a greater degree than all the twentieth-century billboards, commercials, and "Just Say No" speeches combined, and for this he will always be a seminal figure. In the hearts of his family, friends, teammates, and the University of Maryland community, all of whom continue to journey beyond losing a good son, Lenny lives.

He is the breathtaking shooting star.

Through the lessons from Lenny, I was conditioned to accept adversity as another mode of competition. We discovered as teenagers our lives can flip like dimes but being knocked down just means it's time to get up and learn how to stay up. Whatever the situation, own it and win it.

If everything flowed smoothly for me at Maryland, I may have developed other skill sets and become a different man. The rough road we traveled required uncommon perseverance, and perseverance pays.

Suffering through the aftermath takes me into "The League," surviving a scandalous college career gave me the fortitude to survive being shot like a pinball through the NBA for fifteen years, and applying the lessons from the life Lenny lived led to unrivaled success in San Antonio and a world championship finish, light from darkness. The staggering tutorial aged me, hardened me, and robbed me of my innocence, but it also gave me the insight to map the proper route forward.

Len Bias confirms every wise word about becoming the best basketball player you can be. Following him, I discovered even more about being a better man. Reaching us through a game, we commit to memory the ultimate lesson within his legacy.

Remember the power to inspire.

Pursuing Len Bias sheds light on a way to live, and the wide world of professional athletics becomes a career option. Bias rising from Prince George's County to the second pick in the draft says a kid like me can reach the NBA, because Len began to climb while being a typical P.G.

County kid, like me. My father and uncle told me about Elgin Baylor, Dave Bing, and the storied history of Maryland and DC area basketball and still, becoming an NBA player seemed like a fairy tale until Len Bias.

"The Man from Landover" is the identifiable reference of a generation and increases our confidence. Our kids know that there is adversity on the horizon—they also have seen that it can be overcome. Both lessons are essential for the ambitious young ballplayers in the gyms right now.

Len grew from my streets into "The Man" and I looked to him, calculating my chances of being special on the basketball court, too. Len Bias allowed me to trust that success is more than possible, shaping my approach to achievement. I planned to work hard and, by the Grace of God, travel the path.

The most difficult moments in life often have a more profound effect on character than the glory days. At the innermost point of self-analysis, we realize that the hard times were vital for our later success.

I wanted to stand on a soapbox during the summer of 1986 to tell the nation that Lenny Bias was a spiritually conscious, warm-hearted son, a generous big brother, and the best teammate, friend, and counselor a freshman could wish for. But my teenage words would have been hard to hear over all the noise.

On stage, accepting my degree, I thought of grabbing the microphone and screaming, "For you Lenny."

During the post-game press conference after scoring thirty-four points in an NBA game, a fear of mentioning Lenny as my inspiration ties my tongue even though visions of "The Man" flooded my consciousness throughout the contest.

Sitting in a world championship locker room being asked by the media to recap the journey, I hesitated, a fifteen-year professional, worried about telling the truth.

The aftermath of his death prevented me from declaring that his life was a guiding light.

No longer.

Today, I serve as a messenger, deliberate.

Len Bias created a standard and with the social, cognitive, and athletic bars set high, only an exceptional effort receives equal recognition. Attempting to supplant "The Man" as the greatest Terrapin and take his place on the "DMV" Mount Rushmore is like shooting for the sun. Falling short of the distant star leaves the dreamer among the planets in rare space, and Maryland grows into a hotbed for school-age basketball talent.

Case in point: Prince George's County native Kevin Durant said before he ever thought about playing in college or making it to the NBA, his goal was to be the greatest player in his area. That was challenging enough.

Durant proves that being the best in the "DMV" bodes well for success in basketball and beyond.

In 2014, P.G. County and University of Notre Dame standout, 1994 NBA first-round pick, and the New Orleans Pelicans Head Coach Tavares "Monty" Williams says Kevin Durant reminds him of the things Len would have done in the NBA.

Kevin Durant turned twenty-six years old in 2014 and with a lifetime of lessons from a "must win" community, "K.D." impresses like "The Man."

Lenny spurred change, from the playground to the nation's laws, and for some, the debate over his true legacy will be a lifelong exchange. The accurate perspective of all that we can learn from the life of Lenny Bias may allow a level of acceptance most would never have imagined. Though some may forever shake their heads or weep, the possibility exists to think of "The Man" and smile. I do, because I have a clear view beyond the valleys.

I know the legacy of Lenny Bias continually evolves, defined by his teammates, classmates, community, state, country, and the game we love. The University of Maryland and its basketball program grows from Lenny, the tear-watered seed, and therefore Terrapins, their fans, and everyone conscious of our journey will notice Maryland appears to have a permanent Bias.

Being a Marylander and a Terrapin may present a predisposition to protect the legacy of Len Bias. Similar to when a family member makes a mistake or goes astray, the act may be detestable but love embraces the person. When the home team or favorite athlete errs, compassion should flow naturally.

I view the downfall of my sports idol as a trial to overcome, to make things better, and I attack life with the same mindset.

Emerge victorious.

Now old and sentimental, conversations with Terrapin fans expressing an appreciation for my efforts carry me down memory lane. A thoughtful father introduces me to his wide-eyed son and I feel fourteen, looking up at Lenny. A gratifying chat with a blue-chip recruit takes me back to my room in Washington Hall, waking every morning to a hauntingly tangible reminder of the lesson. Being in the building with Coach Williams in Springfield, Massachusetts on the day of his induction into the Naismith Basketball Hall of Fame, and hearing him say the incomparable enshrinement might never have happened without Massenburg and me, melts us, and we remember the quarter-century journey we owe to Len Bias, the shooting star. Accolades go to Len Bias for making us look. We value the reasons we exist. We hope everyone will.

When a dream ends, when a shooting star leaves us breathless, we see the beauty in our time together and the good fortune each day brings. I'm blessed with a wonderful family. I stay connected to Maryland Basketball as a sideline reporter for Terrapin Sports Radio, and in March of 2016 I traveled to my first NCAA Tournament game and tasted the "Sweet Sixteen." Massenburg is still showing Terps how to be champions at the next level. He's a Maryland business owner and doing great work on television covering the Washington Wizards and the NBA. Dreams end and dreams begin.

As the University of Maryland moves through the next era of progress, the **B1G** time, we look forward to serving as examples of an intimate Len Bias lesson for living, creating triumph out of adversity, the legacy of Maryland Basketball we created by forging beyond the loss of a sensational star.

For all we know, Len Bias accomplished everything destined for him to achieve. We cherish having him for twenty-two years to help us navigate the turbulent sea of life.

We are forever grateful to Lenny.

We are Maryland, living with "an inherent Bias."

Disciples of "The Man."

Other Voices

ROBERT "BOB" WADE

University of Maryland Head Basketball Coach, 1986-1989

When Chancellor John Slaughter approached me and ultimately offered me the head coaching position at the University of Maryland months later, I was honored. I knew it was going to be a tough situation in the aftermath of Len Bias passing. There was a dark cloud hovering around the program and, on top of that, I was replacing a beloved legend as the head coach, "Lefty" Driesell.

The most important immediate task facing me was restoring the credibility of the program and the confidence of the team I inherited. I had to earn the players' trust and that was difficult because they didn't know me. I didn't recruit them and didn't have a prior relationship with them. There were a lot of delicate pieces to the puzzle needing to be put together in a very short time.

When I arrived, the players were down in the dumps. The death of Len Bias devastated them. They were his friends, his brothers. They lived together in the dormitories. They were heartbroken. It was such a challenging, stressful, and strenuous time for them.

The credibility of the program and the University had been damaged by the constant media hype. It was an extreme challenge to recruit. Most of the country's best players who would have strongly considered the University of Maryland were no longer interested in playing in College Park at that time. We were trying to heal some very deep wounds and restore the integrity of what was a very tarnished reputation. I am not sure if most people realize the raw wounds and depths of where the program was and how Tony Massenburg, Keith Gatlin, and the 1987-1988 team fought and battled to earn a spot in the NCAA Tournament and advance to the second round just two seasons beyond the tragedy, a phenomenal accomplishment. We navigated through the storm together and formed a very strong bond. We'd come so far in such a short period of time and a ray of hope was on the horizon.

Walt Williams deciding to come to the University of Maryland gave the program instant credibility and a big morale boost showing we could bring in elite talent again. Walt was being recruited by a lot of the top schools in the ACC, and Georgetown as well. He took a leap of faith and put his trust in me and Maryland. Walt was instrumental in changing the direction of the program. He was pivotal to the transition and setting the tone for the eventual long-term success the University enjoys. Maryland, be very proud of the recovery.

NATASHA **CRISS**

Associate Director of the Academic Support and Career Development Unit, University of Maryland Men's Basketball, 1993-1997, 2001-2016

I came to Maryland on my recruiting visit in 1988 well aware of the Len Bias situation. Len had admirers everywhere, in my home state of New Jersey and around the country, and his death resonated throughout amateur athletics. Two years removed from the tragedy, I did not sense doom and gloom as I toured the campus. Institutionally, I am sure coals were being put to the fire, but student life seemed great.

Tony Massenburg was one of the first people I shared a conversation with in "The Quad." Tony and all the student-athletes I met during my visit spoke highly of the program and where things were heading. The atmosphere was so welcoming, I committed to Maryland within minutes of stepping on campus. I found the athletic community to be a close-knit group that really took care of one another—maybe this was a part of the aftermath. No black cloud hovered over the campus. No signs announcing, "These are the post-Bias athletes." We were simply the freshman class of 1988 and I was a member of the Track and Field team, normal.

Every week or two during my first semester, student-athletes took part in seminars and workshops aimed at personal development. A commission formed to define ways to better serve the athletic population, and as a result of their findings a new and required course, Health 140, emerged. The Student Services Division and the Academic Support Unit merged to become the Academic Support and Career Development Unit (ASCDU), a group charged with steering athletes through the educational aspect of being a student-athlete. The administration committed to creating a fostering culture.

Our ASCDU office in Cole Field House had four computers during my time as a student-athlete, shared by the entire athletic community. The University trusted the value of the service provided to the student-athletes and addressed needs when identified. Meeting the needs required expansion, and after graduating I accepted a position within the department to implement and create programs, do community outreach and the most rewarding aspect, work one-on-one with the student-athletes.

We acknowledged and embraced the men's basketball program at Maryland as a sub-culture within the student environment with a unique set of needs. We asked ourselves, "What are the values we are trying to teach them?" As an institution, there are certain values we are trying to instill, as a basketball program, there are things we are trying to instill, and they must cover academically, athletically, socially, every facet of the student-athlete's life. Here are some classes you can take and here is a basketball, now let's win and graduate does not work. There are too many variables and too many things happening. Today, the men's basketball team has an academic counseling team whose sole focus is their success as student-athletes. That is the lesson: its origin may derive from tragic circumstances, but today's student-athlete benefits greatly because of the revision. The seed fell to the ground and now everything is growing.

Len Bias will forever be a Terrapin. His legacy continues to influence the development of programs and services that affect today's student-athletes. From experiencing life as a student-athlete on campus in 1988 through my time as the Career Counselor for the men's basketball team, I have lived the lesson. We persevere. We learn from history and proceed. We do not have to be on the defensive when discussing Len's impact. We continue building, reminding everyone of the resolute Terrapin character.

The University of Maryland suffered during the reflection and recovery phase, but student-athletes choosing College Park become members of a world-class institution celebrated for having the tools necessary to succeed moving forward. We developed a plan for the student-athletes. If they follow the plan, they will graduate. I am a product of the programs and initiatives set forth when heartbreak exposed our flaws. I understand the legacy. We made sure they follow the plan.

JOHNNY **RHODES**

Shooting Guard (1992-1996) and Maryland All-Time Steals Leader

Walt was the attraction. For my friends and me, what mattered most about Maryland was how many "The Wizard" scored. Walt did what everyone on the playground saw "Magic" Johnson doing in the NBA. "The Wizard" brought the ball up the court, set up what he wanted people to think was an offense, because everyone knew he was shooting it, made the best pass of the game, got the biggest rebound, had a highlight dunk, and scored the most points. I really cannot remember the losses. His style of play and Walt being a local talent made Maryland an attractive option for me. When I visited campus on my recruiting trip, I found Walt to be a regular, cool kid from Crossland who just happened to play basketball exceptionally well. Also, his P.G. was like DC.

Massenburg was just a beast. He looked like an NBA player on television and the day I met him. Power and speed, good hands, good touch, crazy hops, Tony was a true big man and played a game I knew nothing about. Walt was a big guard. I could relate.

Walt shined like a star for sure but Tony and all the Terps liked him because he was just Walt. We talked about playing together for one season and forming the best senior-freshman backcourt in college basketball. I was super excited about the DC-P.G. County connection, an "All-Met" tandem at Maryland. I saw us pressing for forty minutes and playing a fast-paced game, like we were playing at Dunbar, DC. I told Walt to count me in. I left campus committed. One thing: If I wanted to be a Terp, I needed to go to prep school for a year. And, I wanted to be a Terp. So, I had to abandon my dreams of playing with "The Wizard," but I think he did okay without me.

Walt stayed in touch with me during my prep year and I followed the Terps closely. Coaches from everywhere called to see if I changed my decision on committing to Maryland but I never wavered. Walt scored thirty every night and I watched the highlights, imagining playing in Cole Field House among family and friends like "Wiz." That was his thing when we talked: The joys of playing before a home crowd and being recognized for uplifting your community was what Len Bias did and Walt did well following his lead. I could do that. I wanted to do that.

The competitor in me hated Duane Simpkins and Exree Hipp. Off the court, those guys were great. Our first conversation about forming a trio at Maryland happened at a DC summer league event. I was committed to College Park and each of us loved Walt's game and the brand of basketball Maryland played. Talk of the Michigan "Fab Five" galvanized our three-piece around the opportunity to stay at home where family and friends can see every game. "Simp" and "X" said, "Let's do it," and we took off. Coach Williams adds Mario Lucas, a modern-day stretch-forward, and six-ten center Nemanja Petrovic to round out our freshmen five. Joe Smith and Keith Booth join us in 1993 and the ball starts rolling. "Petro" transferred to Saint Joseph's University, won All-Academic honors, and made it to the "Sweet Sixteen." Sadly, on Thursday, June 19, 2008, twenty-two years to the day Len Bias passed away, Nemanja lost his battle with a viral infection and left us way too soon.

Walt, Tony, Derrick and Cedric Lewis, and the guys before us always played hard and fearless regardless of what was going on or the competition, and the fans always supported that kind of effort. All of us felt the hurt from Len's demise. My grade school coaches made frequent references to the great rise and fall. The veteran Terps that came after Len did a great job creating an atmosphere and a way of playing that enabled Maryland to begin the process of moving forward. Every youngster who went to College Park during the summer and was lucky enough to get the chance to play with those guys quickly discovered a higher level of competitiveness. Being true professionals, Walt, Tony, and those guys came back home and schooled us, and we took everything we gained and gave it to the NCAA: A family affair.

Seeing Joe and Keith standing strong during the summer games showed us we could compete with anyone and, by March of our first season together, we had sincere aspirations of winning it all. Maryland Basketball survived and we demanded a return to excellence. We were able to lay the framework for classes to follow and dance in the "Sweet Sixteen," which makes the Final Four attainable. I was playing professionally overseas when the young Terps won the national championship and I made sure it was a worldwide celebration. Terps on top.

ANNE **TURKOS**

Archivist, University of Maryland

I remember exactly where I stood and how I found out about the death of Len Bias, as so many people do. In fact, three decades later, I still think about that shocking telephone call every time I pass the office in McKeldin Library where I worked that afternoon. Relatively new to the University of Maryland at the time, having joined the UMD Libraries' staff in January 1985, I was not as fervent a follower of Terrapin men's basketball as I am now. But I knew even then without a doubt the tragedy unfolding that beautiful June day would have a profound impact on our entire campus.

As the weeks passed under the glare of intense media scrutiny, the University suffered hit after hit as significant problems surfaced with the academic achievement of Maryland athletes (and not just in basketball), a flourishing drug culture, and coaches and administrators who could not or would not take the actions necessary to make needed improvements in Terrapin athletics. No stone was left unturned, and UMD remained in the news for months and months. The sadness resulting from Len's tragic choice that morning consumed the entire campus and still has a deep effect on our collective psyche.

Are we a stronger institution because of this horrible nightmare? I firmly believe so, and it is hard to imagine what the University would be like if it had not examined and improved every aspect of its operation in the years following that fateful day.

The legend of Len Bias lives on. Each year, in the University Archives, we receive numerous requests for photos of Len or footage from games in which he played. UMD students of today research and write about the impact of his death on their alma mater and the world. University image-makers and administrators are still haunted by this watershed event in our history. It is the news story that will never completely disappear, and, in many ways, that is a positive for our campus. It is a constant reminder that we need to stop and think about what we are doing and the effect our words and deeds will have on the UMD community, our state, the nation, and the world. Len was an amazing basketball player, and his memory is a touchstone for all who knew him or watched him on the court. We should never forget what he meant to the University of Maryland while we continue to practice the lessons learned from his death.

Afterword

TONY MASSENBURG **AND WALT WILLIAMS**

The image on the front cover of this book illustrates the considerable reach of Len Bias. He was by my side when I scored the first points of my Terrapin career and he showed me the way to anchor the difficult post for Maryland, with an assist from "The Wizard." Walt handles the press, resets the offense and, while being double-teamed, pulls up and drains a three-pointer, allowing Gary Williams and the Terrapins to apply full-court pressure. Johnny Rhodes steals the ball and zips it ahead to Keith Booth who lobs an alley-oop to Joe Smith which puts Maryland back on top. The Williams-led Terps finish the first half strong and reach the midway point with a sizable advantage. Maryland opens the second half perfectly from the field with a succession of talented recruits building an insurmountable lead. Juan Dixon caps the quest for a championship with a dominating performance, winning the admiration of a nation, affording Maryland fans the freedom to live happily, and with perspective, ever after.

In the lower right corner of the image on the front cover is Duke Blue Devil Jay Bilas, now an ESPN Analyst. Bilas and his college teammate Johnny Dawkins, the Washington, DC native and 1986 Naismith College Player of the Year, witnessed Lenny's four-year rise first hand. Dawkins, the current head coach at the University of Central Florida, emphasized the essence of Lenny's persuasion by stating that he's been looking for the last twenty-five years and has never seen a player who reminds him of Bias.

The search is timelessly significant and speaks to Len's long-term impact. Dawkins and Bilas are widely regarded as two of the brightest minds in college basketball today and as they evaluate talent from coast to coast and around the globe, their first-hand knowledge of Len's unique abilities remains a discriminative factor. In their youth, Dawkins and Bilas faced the two-time ACC Player of the Year, and, although they would love to announce another of the caliber of the "Man from Landover," they haven't seen anyone who could reach Lenny's level.

Former NBA Head Coach "Monty" Williams, on the other hand, identified Kevin Durant as such an outstanding player, a man who could enhance Lenny's legend and his posthumous influence on a generation. Striving to leap Lenny Bias remains a tall task, as Coach Johnny Dawkins and other dignitaries will confirm, but the reward is well worth the effort.

Minutes after the announcement of Coach Williams retiring in 2011, we connected by telephone to share disbelief. The news takes us to Cole Field House, to June of 1989 when Coach first calls us together. Twenty-five years after Lenny, the Williams-led mission to revive Maryland reaches completion. And now, a quarter of a century beyond our first conversation, the University of Maryland commands global respect, national champion banners hang for the men's and women's basketball programs, and the Terps are well positioned to attract talent from the ultra-competitive "DMV" and all over the world. The torch passed, glowing brightly, red.

Describing the decision-making process that led to the team MVP award being named in honor of Len Bias, Maryland's Head Coach offers the following perspective:

> *"I asked for a list of former players. Len Bias is the greatest basketball player ever at the University of Maryland, and that was that: The Len Bias Award."*
>
> *—Mark Turgeon, University of Maryland Head Basketball Coach*

Fittingly, the 2013 recipient of the Len Bias Award, Alex Len, wears number twenty-five, punctuating the onset of our twenty-five-year march as Terrapin teammates. Alex. Len.

The 2014 Len Bias Award winner is "Dez" Wells, a North Carolina native schooled in the greatness of Lenny Bias with gratitude for the contributions of Terrapins past.

Crowning the quarter-century voyage, the University of Maryland invites Dr. Lonise Bias, Len's mother, to speak at the Memorial Chapel on a picturesque Sunday morning and we embraced the memory and the message we share moving forward, with love.

A few months later, Maryland recognizes "Lefty" Driesell with a halftime salute and a bronze bas-relief, and Terrapins of all ages unite, shaping the legacy into the lessons from Lenny. Sitting with the charismatic Charles G. Driesell as he fills the room with the best of Leonard Bias, watching him see his banner being added to the Xfinity Center rafters, and posing beside the sculpture commemorating his Hall of Fame coaching career adds an exclamation point to the reasons Maryland seized our attention three decades ago. Seventeen and dreaming of teaming with Bias in College Park, Massenburg absorbed the tantalizing Terrapin tales narrated by "The Left-hander" and followed his heart to Maryland. Sharing the legacy during our two years together as Terrapins added fuel to our faith and served as a foundation to leap toward achievement.

We hold on to the warm feelings of joy and pride that come from Coach Driesell's story-telling, standing arm in arm with him and Coach Williams in Cole Field House, celebrating the final "Midnight Madness" as a member of the ACC, from "Dez" Wells crediting Len Bias as a catalyst for the current era, and P.G. County's own "Melo" Trimble saying Maryland was the only school for him. It recaptures the virtue we celebrated as youngsters wanting to be "The Man." The revitalizing spirit of togetherness within the Terrapin family keeps us moving forward, fearless.

We thank and appreciate Coach Williams for growing Maryland Basketball and penning an eloquent foreword for the LESSONS FROM LENNY. In the same breath, we thank and appreciate Coach Driesell for launching Maryland Basketball and providing the closing sentiments to forward our message. Remembering Len Bias living an inspirational twenty-two years facilitates journeying beyond that one cruel moment.

We thank our alma mater for honoring the life of Len Bias with a place among the immortals in the University of Maryland Athletics Hall of Fame. Finally, to the students and fans wearing the Bias number thirty-four jersey, we see you. You're the greatest!

FINAL WORD

CHARLES "LEFTY" **DRIESELL**

NAISMITH MEMORIAL BASKETBALL HALL OF FAME COACH

I loved Leonard Bias like a son, always will. And the University of Maryland should always love Len too. Leonard was a Christian, family-first, caring young man who died in a terrible accident, but that awful occasion does not erase all of the good in his remarkable life.

Leonard Bias is a credit to the University of Maryland, just the third Terrapin to win the ACC Athlete of the Year Award following John Lucas and Renaldo Nehemiah. And some of the best players to attend Maryland after his accidental death chose College Park because of their admiration for Leonard and the basketball program he helped build. Walt Williams, Keith Booth, Steve Francis, Juan Dixon—guys who grew up in Maryland and now have their jerseys hanging from the rafters, and "Dez" Wells, a leader at Maryland and winner of the Len Bias Award for team MVP all refer to Leonard as an inspiration. And Karl-Anthony Towns, the first pick in the NBA draft and unanimous 2016 Rookie of the Year, a McDonald's High School All-American, Gatorade Player of the Year and Dean's List student from New Jersey, a kid, calls Len Bias his favorite player, showing the powerful influence Leonard continues having on the youth of today.

Len Bias also inspires those of us who were fortunate enough to share time with him. I am proud of having had four years to be a part of his life, to coach him, and see him grow from a well-raised teenager into a wonderful young man. Tony Massenburg and his teammates have fond memories of playing with the two-time ACC Player of the Year, his compassionate nature, and undeniable affection for College Park and the Terrapin family. Leonard was a good person, a joy, a transitioning student-athlete who realized basketball opened doors to a grand and secure future for him and his family. Like many young adults, he anticipated having the chance to return to the University of Maryland and complete the requirements for his degree while at the same time earning a fine living playing the game he loved. Given the option to focus on a lucrative career, many people consider taking time away from studies to answer a golden opportunity knocking. Sadly, Len succumbs to a horrible accident and we must learn to live in the absence of a dear friend and favorite son.

I appreciate Tony and Walt reminding everyone Leonard Bias lives at the University of Maryland and in the heart of the Terrapin basketball program. His family loves him; every Terrapin fan I know loves Len Bias; Maryland Basketball is shaped by his legend; his peers speak of him with the highest regard, and, through the lessons, people discover how to live stronger.

I miss Leonard. I think of him plenty. Tony and I smile telling stories about our good friend and the good that stems from his life. The tears that form in Walt's eyes as he describes wanting to follow Len to Maryland reveal his mighty impact. We can celebrate the life of Len Bias, an excellent son, devoted teammate, serious student, promising artist, superior athlete, all-time Maryland great, and extraordinarily influential human being. Celebrate the amazing life, the gift in the memory of a very special young man.

By the Numbers

LEN **BIAS**

University of Maryland, Career Numbers

- ACC Player of the Year (1985 & 1986)
- Player of the Year – District 3-B (1985 & 1986) – selected by U.S. Basketball Writers Association
- Unanimous selection to All-District 3-B Team
- 1st Team All-ACC (1985 & 1986)
- 1st Team All-American – Associated Press/NABC/NBWA/UPI/ Naismith (1986)
- 2nd Team All-American – Associated Press/Basketball Weekly (1985)
- 3rd Team All-American – National Association of Basketball Coaches (1985)
- Alaska Shootout All-Tournament Team
- ACC All-Tournament Team (1984)
- MVP of ACC Tournament (1984)
- John Wooden Award finalist (1985)
- Naismith Trophy finalist (1985)
- NBC-TV Player of the Game for UMD vs. Villanova (1/27/85)
- Led ACC in scoring (1985)
- Led ACC in scoring and free throw percentage (1986)

SEASON	GP	FGM	FGA	PCT.	FTM	FTA	.PCT	REB.	ASST.	PTS.
FRESHMAN	30	86	180	.478	42	66	.636	125	22	217
SOPHOMORE	32	211	372	.567	66	86	.767	145	48	488
JUNIOR	37	274	519	.530	153	197	.777	251	65	701
SENIOR	32	267	491	.544	209	242	.864	224	33	743

Len Bias held the following records at the end of his college career:

- Most points scored in an away game: 41 vs. Duke (1/25/86) – currently tied with Vasquez
- Most points in a season: 743 (1985-86) and 708 (1984-85) – currently stands at #2 and #5 all-time
- Most career points: 2149 – currently stands at #3
- Most 30-point games in a season: 5 – currently stands at #2
- Most 30-point games in a career: 6 – currently stands at #3
- Most 20-point games in a season: 24 – currently stands at #2
- Most double-figure games in a season: 36 – still holds record
- Most double-figure games in a career: 108 – currently stands at #3
- Season free throws made: 209 – currently tied at #2
- Career free throws made: 470 – currently stands at #2
- Career games: 131 – currently tied at #11
- Season minutes: 1352 – still holds record
- Career minutes: 4302 – currently stands at #3
- Season minutes per game: 37.0 – currently stands at #2

TONY **MASSENBURG**

University of Maryland, Career Numbers

- 2nd Team All-ACC (1990)
- 3rd Team All-ACC – Associated Press (1989)
- Honorable Mention All-ACC – Atlantic Coast Sports Writers Association (1989)
- MVP at Freedom Bowl Classic (1989)
- All-Tournament Team at Freedom Bowl Classic (1989)
- All-Tournament Team at Sun Bowl Classic (1989)

SEASON	G	FG	FGA	FG%	FT%	TRB	AST	STL	BLK	PTS
1985-86	29	28	56	.500	.563	60	0	9	11	83
1987-88	23	93	179	.520	.573	122	10	9	22	233
1988-89	29	197	358	.550	.600	226	21	15	27	481
1989-90	31	206	408	.505	.721	314	20	28	37	557
CAREER	112	524	1001	.523	.643	722	51	61	97	1354

- ACC All-Tournament Team (1989 & 1990)
- ACC Player of the Week honors (1990)
- Led team in scoring, rebounding, and field goal percentage (1989)
- Led team in rebounding (1990) and #2 in ACC for rebounds per game (1990)
- Career high 34 points vs. Georgia Tech (2/3/90)
- 1 of only 2 ACC players in 1990 to average double figures in scoring and rebounding
- 1990 2nd Team All-ACC Selection

SEASON	G	MP	FG	FGA	FG%	FT%	TRB	AST	STL	BLK	PTS
1985-86	29	12.0	1.0	1.9	.500	.563	2.1	0.0	0.3	0.4	2.9

SEASON	G	MP	FG	FGA	FG%	FT%	TRB	AST	STL	BLK	PTS
1987-88	23	26.8	4.0	7.8	.520	.573	5.3	0.4	0.4	1.0	10.1
1988-89	29	34.5	6.8	12.3	.550	.600	7.8	0.7	0.5	0.9	16.6
1989-90	31	31.4	6.6	13.2	.505	.721	10.1	0.6	0.9	1.2	18.0
CAREER	112	26.2	4.7	8.9	.523	.643	6.4	0.5	0.5	0.9	12.1

Tony Massenberg held the following records at the end of his college career:

- Season offensive rebounds (120) – currently stands at #4
- Career offensive rebounds (270) – currently stands at #6
- Season offensive rebounds per game (3.9) – currently stands at #2
- Career offensive rebounds per game (2.4) – currently stands at #6

WALT **WILLIAMS**

University of Maryland, Career Numbers

- 1st Team All-American – Scripps Howard/Los Angeles Athletic Club/Basketball Times (1992)
- 2nd Team All-American – Associated Press (1992)
- 1st Team All-ACC (1992)
- ACC Player of the Week honors (1992)
- ACC All-Tournament Team (1992)
- U.S. National Team – Pan American Games (1991)
- MVP at ECAC Holiday Festival (1990)
- Wooden Award finalist (1992)
- Naismith Player of the Year finalist (1992)
- Only ACC player to rank in top 10 in assists, steals, and blocks (1990)
- Held a nation-best 7-game streak of 30 or more points (1992)
- Led all ACC players in scoring (1992)
- Led team in free throw percentage (1990 & 1991)
- Led team in points per game (1991 & 1992)
- 1991 Pan American Games Record (Steals)
- Scored 30 points or more in 7 consecutive ACC games
- 1992 All-ACC 1st Team and Scripps-Howard 1st Team All-American

SEASON	G	FG	FGA	FG%	3P%	FT%	TRB	AST	STL	BLK	PTS
1988-89	26	75	170	.441	.259	.623	92	66	33	13	190
1989-90	33	143	296	.483	.448	.776	138	149	57	34	420
1990-91	17	109	243	.449	.295	.837	86	91	25	6	318
1991-92	29	256	542	.472	.371	.758	162	104	60	28	776
CAREER	105	583	1251	.466	.359	.762	478	410	175	81	1704

SEASON	G	FG	FGA	FG%	3P%	FT%	TRB	AST	STL	BLK	PTS
1988-89	26	2.9	6.5	.441	.259	.623	3.5	2.5	1.3	0.5	7.3
1989-90	33	4.3	9.0	.483	.448	.776	4.2	4.5	1.7	1.0	12.7
1990-91	17	6.4	14.3	.449	.295	.837	5.1	5.4	1.5	0.4	18.7
1991-92	29	8.8	18.7	.472	.371	.758	5.6	3.6	2.1	1.0	26.8
CAREER	105	5.6	11.9	.466	.359	.762	4.6	3.9	1.7	0.8	16.2

Walt Williams held the following records at the end of his college career:

- Points in a season (776) – record still stands
- Scoring average in a season (26.8) – record still stands
- Career steals (175) – currently stands at #9
- Steals in a game (7) – currently tied for #7
- Season field goal attempts (542) – record still stands
- Season 3-point baskets made (89) – currently stands at #3
- Career 3-point baskets made (154) – currently stands at #9
- Season 3-point basket attempts (240) – record still stands
- Career 3-point basket attempts (429) – currently stands at #9
- Most 3-point baskets in a game (7) vs. FSU (2/5/92) – record broken by Mike Jones in 2006
- Most 30-point games in a season (11) – record still stands
- Most 30-point games in a career (14) – record still stands
- Most 20-point games in a season (26) – record still stands

TONY **MASSENBURG**

NBA Career Season Averages

- 2005 NBA World Champion

YEAR	TEAM	G	FG%	3P%	FT%	RPG	APG	SPG	BPG	PPG
1990-91	San Antonio	35	.450	.000	.622	1.7	0.1	0.1	0.3	2.3
1991-92	San Antonio	1	.200	.000	.000	0.0	0.0	0.0	0.0	2.0
1991-92	Char-lotte	3	.000	.000	.500	1.3	0.0	0.3	0.0	0.3
1991-92	Boston	7	.444	.000	.500	1.3	0.0	0.0	0.1	1.4
1991-92	Golden State	7	.625	.000	.667	1.7	0.0	0.0	0.0	2.3
1991-92	-	18	.400	.000	.600	1.4	0.0	0.1	0.1	1.6
1994-95	L.A. Clippers	80	.469	.000	.753	5.7	0.8	0.6	0.7	9.3
1995-96	Toronto	24	.510	.000	.662	6.9	0.8	0.5	0.4	10.1
1995-96	Phila-delphia	30	.483	.000	.739	6.2	0.4	0.5	0.4	9.9
1995-96	-	54	.495	.000	.707	6.5	0.6	0.5	0.4	10.0
1996-97	New Jersey	79	.485	.000	.631	6.5	0.3	0.5	0.6	7.2
1997-98	Van-couver	61	.479	.000	.730	3.8	0.3	0.4	0.4	6.5
1998-99	Van-couver	43	.487	.000	.665	6.0	0.5	0.6	0.9	11.2
1999-00	Houston	10	.444	.000	.875	2.7	0.3	0.2	0.5	4.6
2000-01	Van-couver	52	.462	.000	.700	4.0	0.2	0.2	0.5	4.5
2001-02	Mem-phis	73	.456	1.000	.718	4.4	0.4	0.4	0.4	5.5
2002-03	Utah	58	.448	.000	.774	2.7	0.3	0.3	0.3	4.7

YEAR	TEAM	G	FG%	3P%	FT%	RPG	APG	SPG	BPG	PPG
2003-04	Sacra-mento	59	.475	.000	.683	3.2	0.5	0.2	0.3	4.3
2004-05	San Antonio	61	.407	.000	.762	2.7	0.2	0.3	0.3	3.2
CAREER		683	.470	.091	.705	4.3	0.4	0.4	0.4	6.2

*1992-93 Reggio Emilia, Italy. 1992-93 Malaga, Spain. 1993-94 Barcelona, Spain.

WALT **WILLIAMS**

NBA Career Season Averages

- 1997 NBA All-Star 3-Point Shootout 1st Round Winner

YEAR	TEAM	G	FG%	3P%	FT%	RPG	APG	SPG	BPG	PPG
1992-93	Sacra-mento	59	.435	.319	.742	4.5	3.0	1.1	0.5	17.0
1993-94	Sacra-mento	57	.390	.288	.635	4.1	2.3	0.9	0.4	11.2
1994-95	Sacra-mento	77	.446	.348	.731	4.5	4.1	1.6	0.8	16.4
1995-96	Sacra-mento	45	.435	.341	.756	4.6	3.7	1.2	0.9	14.6
1995-96	Miami	28	.463	.455	.550	4.0	2.3	1.1	0.6	12.0
1995-96	-	73	.444	.389	.703	4.4	3.2	1.2	0.8	13.6
1996-97	Toronto	73	.427	.400	.765	5.0	2.7	1.3	0.8	16.4
1997-98	Toronto	28	.392	.380	.817	4.2	2.5	1.4	0.8	12.4
1997-98	Portland	31	.378	.344	.908	2.6	1.7	0.6	0.4	8.4
1997-98	-	59	.386	.365	.864	3.4	2.1	1.0	0.6	10.3
1998-99	Portland	48	.424	.438	.832	3.0	1.7	0.8	0.6	9.3
1999-00	Houston	76	.458	.391	.821	4.0	2.1	0.6	0.6	10.9
2000-01	Houston	72	.394	.395	.770	3.4	1.3	0.4	0.4	8.3
2001-02	Houston	48	.419	.426	.784	3.4	1.4	0.4	0.2	9.4
2002-03	Dallas	66	.393	.374	.620	3.1	0.9	0.6	0.4	5.5
CAREER		708	.425	.379	.743	3.9	2.3	0.9	0.5	11.8

THE UNIVERSITY OF MARYLAND, COLLEGE PARK
Ranks 40th among the Best Global Universities

October 2016, U.S. News & World Report
(Comparison of 1000 Schools in 65 Countries)

SOURCES

This book reflects our ongoing conversation with the University of Maryland family concerning the journey beyond the loss of our friend and role model, Len Bias. Measuring his influential life professionally, personally, confidentially, and with strangers for more than a quarter of a century strengthens our Terrapin shell. Each chat advances the LESSONS FROM LENNY, and we thank one and all. We reviewed hundreds of magazine and newspaper articles, game tapes, and documentaries to shape the book, most notably:

- ABC/ESPN
- CBS Sports
- NBC Sports
- Sporting News
- Sports Illustrated
- The Baltimore Sun
- The Chicago Tribune
- The Los Angeles Times
- The New York Times
- The Palm Beach Post
- The USA Today
- The Washington Post
- The Washington Times
- The University of Maryland, College Park

Extensive Internet searches uncovered an abundance of useful websites including, but not limited to:

- basketball-reference.com
- bbc.co.uk
- bleacherreport.com
- boston.com
- btn.com
- celticslife.com
- cnn.com
- courttv.com

- csnwashington.com
- cstv.com
- examiner.com
- famm.org
- house.gov
- huffingtonpost.com
- insidehoops.com
- nba.com
- ncaa.com
- newsok.com
- nj.com
- oregonlive.com
- pressboxonline.com
- scrippsnews.com
- shanghairanking.com
- spurstalk.com
- theacc.com
- thesentinel.com
- waukesha.patch.com
- usabasketball.com
- ussc.gov

Several books of note influenced LESSONS FROM LENNY:

- *Legends of Maryland Basketball, Tales from the Maryland Terrapins, and Born Ready*, by Dave Ungrady,
- *Never Too Young to Die* by Lewis Cole,
- *Lenny, Lefty, and the Chancellor* by C. Fraser Smith,
- *Sweet Redemption* by Gary Williams and David A. Vise,
- *Bigger Than the Game* by Michael Weinreb,
- *Shooting Stars* by LeBron James and Buzz Bissinger,
- *The Book of Basketball* by Bill Simmons.

We greatly appreciate the work of the nameless reporters, writers, authors, editors, publishers, and members of the media whose diligence impacts the book. Please forgive any inadvertent omissions.

—Tony Massenburg and Walt Williams

ACKNOWLEDGMENTS

First, we give thanks to God. Looking back at the critical moments in life, wondering how did we survive or succeed in this situation, every time the answer is God.

Thank you, Bias family. We wrote LESSONS FROM LENNY as a testament to the remarkably inspirational *life* of Len Bias.

From the start, University of Maryland Archivist Anne Turkos worked around the clock to answer every request. We thank Mrs. Turkos and the gracious souls joining us on the mission to publish our lessons from Lenny, including but not limited to: Charles "Lefty" Driesell, Robert "Bob" Wade, Gary Williams, Mark Turgeon, and their staffs for insight and Terrapin direction.

Dr. Wallace Loh, Dr. Ann Wylie, Dr. Mona Levine, Pam Phillips, Natasha Criss, Kevin Glover, Kenny Beaver, Cleo Long-Thomas, Troy Wainwright, Nicole Pollard, Sammy Popat, Justin Moore, Jonathan Trock, Amanda K. Hawk, Shannon Saia and Zach Bolno for Terrapin family support.

Marc Rosendorf, Bill Mandir, Leigh Ann Lindquist, and Charles Siegel for thorough legal guidance.

Conferences with Hank Lewis, David A. Vise, Ronald Goldfarb, and Robert L. Clayton validated our personal confidence in the worth of LESSONS FROM LENNY. Consulting with distinguished analyst Dan Bonner broadened our perception.

Dana Steinberg and Terry Irving fashioned our thoughts with editorial expertise. Pilar Afanador Ruiz assisted in creating fantastic artwork. Ted Bowman, Lianne Hepler and Adam Robinson generously gave us their veteran publishing and design counsel. Shockoe Studios delivered first-class website development. Our special appreciation extends to Len Elmore, Johnny Rhodes, Steve Blake, Keith Booth, Juan Dixon, Dezmine Wells, Romelo Trimble, and our brotherhood: Maryland Basketball. Whyde Range Productions receives high regard for brilliant foresight, research, and ingenuity, and, we recognize with praise the countless, priceless conversations.

TONY

Alvin and Hattie Massenburg worked and sacrificed for me to have every imaginable opportunity. I thank my parents for providing, for leading by example in everything from competition to compassion. I love you with all my heart and depend on your exemplary parenting template to guide T.J and Jordan. I love my sons, they are my world, and my parents shaped my universe. I aim at being for T.J. and Jordan the anchor of love my parents present for me.

Without my grandmother Christine, the center of our family, no one exists. I love you, along with all my aunts, uncles, and cousins. Your support gives me strength. I offer gratefulness to my grade school coaches and teachers for stressing hard work and best effort, and my high school teammates who bleed Sussex County. We win! My freshman classmates of 1985, the original boys-to-men in the aftermath, encourage me every day.

Walt and I express the highest degree of respect and gratitude to Dr. Lonise Bias, for wrapping her arms around us as our world crumbled in June of 1986, and for the embrace we share living the lessons. God bless you all.

WALT

Dearest to my heart, I thank my wife April Williams and my three sons Tyrese, Kamari, and Bryce. My love for you and my determination to provide your heart's desire inspires me in everything I do. Without you, I am lost. The unconditional love my Mom has for my sister and me, both of whom I love beyond measure, provides a wealth of self-assurance persuading us to believe we can be anything we want, and this mindset spearheads my effort from childhood, and will enrich my life forever! I thank my sister Stephanie who demanded I put in the work necessary to blossom. Without her tough love, I may never have reached the NBA.

I love, thank, and genuinely appreciate my coaches, teammates, DC/P.G. County kin, cherished relatives in North Carolina, Beaumont, and Akron, and "My Boys." Family is everything and our closeness are the values I hope to instill in my sons. I honor my Dad, Aunt Pauline, Uncle Hervey, Aunt Lula, Carrie Lee, and my family members no longer with us.

Len Bias: Rest in peace.

To all of you: Your support has given me great confidence throughout my life, knowing so many people care for me regardless of whether I succeed. The result of love like this is never fearing to fail at anything I attempt.

Thank you for showing me the way.

INDEX